SILENCE !
THE COURT IS IN SESSION

Translated by
Priya Adarkar

OXFORD
UNIVERSITY PRESS

OXFORD
UNIVERSITY PRESS

Oxford University Press is a department of the University of Oxford.
It furthers the University s objective of excellence in research, scholarship,
and education by publishing worldwide. Oxford is a registered trade mark of
Oxford University Press in the UK and in certain other countries

Published in India by
Oxford University Press
YMCA Library Building, 1, Jai Singh Road, New Delhi 110001, India

ISBN-13: 978-0-19-560313-2
ISBN-10: 0-19-560313-3

27th impression 2013

Printed in India by De Unique, New Delhi 110 018

INTRODUCTION

SHANTATA! COURT CHALU AHE is in some respects typical of
Tendulkar's writings. The experience of the play, as is usual
with him, stems not from a concept but a real incident. In
this particular case the stimulus came from an amateur
group on its way to stage a mock trial in Vile Parle (the
suburb where Tendulkar lives) ; the bits of conversation
he heard as he guided the members to their destination sug-
gested the outline of the play. Secondly, in the actual writing of a work, Tendulkar is invariably conditioned by pres-
sures from directors, actors and friends. The play was written for *Rangayan* at the instance of Arvind and Sulabha
Deshpande and even two days prior to the performance
the final draft could not be said to have been completed.

But, in another sense, the play appears uncharacteristic
of Tendulkar. In his earlier works he had dwelt on the
woes of the middle class with a degree of sympathy, border-
ing on sentiment. With *Shantata* came a parting of ways.
The transformation is difficult to explain. The change was
possibly the result of a deep personal experience. For, on
the one hand, it unleashed characters (Benare, Sakharam,
Ghasiram) in a state of collision with accepted norms and,
on the other, it revealed ineffectual middle class types with
an ugly, vicious leer lurking under a smug surface.

All this might, of course, sound like hindsight today.
When the play was staged, ten years ago to be precise, it
was received no differently than the usual Tendulkar play
entered for the Annual State Drama Competition. In fact,
it never even made the finals. The Jury was probably in-
fluenced by one of its members who is reported to have
declared, 'This cannot be described as a play.' But undeter-
red by this setback, *Rangayan* went on to do thirty-five performances, risking a loss of six thousand rupees in the bar-
gain. But the play did have an impact. In the following
year Satyadev Dubey (Theatre Unit) produced it in Hindi
and this time it carried the day at the competition with
Sulabha Deshpande winning the prizes for both direction and
acting. In 1970, Tendulkar was awarded the Kamladevi

Chattopadhyay Award and *Shantata* was adjudged 'The Play of the Year.' In 1971, he won the Sangeet Natak Akademi's Award for Playwriting. *Shantata* was translated into several languages. Tripti Mitra, the eminent actress, appeared in the main role in the Bengali version. A little later the play was made into a film by Satyadev Dubey with support from the Film Finance Corporation. The BBC broadcast it in English. There were in all more than 150 performances in Marathi and, after the first thirty-five shows, *Rangayan* could always count on a good house and even some profit.

Shantata brought Tendulkar recognition on a national scale. He came to be regarded with Mohan Rakesh, Badal Sircar and Girish Karnad as a leading force in a national theatre movement.

Obviously audiences were in a mood to listen to a playwright ready to fix a remorseless gaze on the contradictions within a personality, even the most insignificant one, a playwright who refused to offer easy legal remedies to social problems or to pin his faith on a change of heart in men. Acutely conscious of the violent impulses behind a respectable facade and of the overwhelming compulsions of sex, he could place his discoveries within a recognizably Indian context, essentially middle class, and rooted. His long association with the theatre had yielded dividends. It had taught him to mould this familiar material into dramatic shape.

Today it is easy to detect the craft that went into the plotting of the play. It is conceived as a game and the idea that all that is happening on the stage is part-mock, part-earnest gives it a 'theatrical' edge. The mock-element is all-pervasive. What we are witnessing is a mere enactment of what is a rehearsal of sorts of nothing more than a mock-trial to be staged later in the day. Nowadays the game-sequence appears frequently enough in a play. It lifts the performance somewhat since it offers so much scope for uninhibited physical movement, for horse-play. Even so, it is, for the most part, little more than an inset. But in

Shantata the play and its structure revolve wholly round the idea of a game and include the essential ingredient of 'reversal'. Benare, who is on the offensive in the beginning, finds herself trapped at the close of the play. The innocuous latch which has hurt her finger and drawn her blood (as she enters the place) later shuts the group in and, in fact, takes on the dimension of a barricade. The claustrophobic atmosphere inside becomes the kind of setting where social masks are shed.

When the members of the troupe entered the room, we half-expected banter and cordiality, as among friends. Banter there was, but alongside a strong streak of pettiness. Perhaps for them theatre activity had reduced itself to an escape from personal disappointments! Benare lets out that Sukhatme is, in real life, a lawyer without a brief ; here he will be seen bursting to exhibit his knowledge of the legal process. Sukhatme for his part, has a dig at Karnik's so called grasp of 'intimate' theatre. Supported, by Balu Rokde, he riles at the unfortunate Ponkshe, who has, actually failed his Inter Science Exams but professes during the trial to be an expert on scientific affairs. Ponkshe, in turn, jeers at Rokde for his total dependence on the Kashikars. And the group unites to ridicule the absurd gestures of mutual devotion made by the couple and also their childlessness. The whole lot of them try to needle Benare but at least in the first half of the play she is able to out-smart them. The name of Prof. Damle, who has failed to turn up, hovers in the air, giving rise to some inexplicable uneasiness.

They have plenty of time to kill before the performance. So they pick on the expedient of initiating the local chap Samant into the intricacies of Court procedure and later using him as a replacement. Benare will be on trial ; after all it is nothing more than a harmless game.

But before long the game begins to assume a grim aspect. The accusations against Benare are based partly on conjecture, partly on hearsay. But the darts strike home. She has tried to seduce almost every male present, lure him into marriage. Ironically enough, it is the local 'innocent' who delivers the final blow. In his excitement, he reads out a passage from a novel. The details seem to fit Benare's case. (Here is a typical instance of someone, poor in experience, feeding his own imagination with popular reading fare. It is a subject to which Tendulkar returns in *Baby*, but from a different angle.)

The door latch has long since fallen into place. The group has by now safely insulated itself. What began as a game has evolved into a hunt. Benare is the quarry and the group, accuser and judge rolled into one. The sentence meted out to her is savage: the infant in her womb must be destroyed ; she must lose her teaching job, her only source of livelihood. There is no mention of the 'intellectual' who abandoned her, the absent Damle.

Having created this situation, the playwright seems to have had no other option except to allow Benare her say. Her inert frame stirs a little to communicate to us what she knows about men who profess love but, in fact, only hunger for the flesh. Perhaps a realization such as this (which also embodies an awareness of the cravings of her own body) needed a better dramatic equivalent. As it stands, the soliloquy sounds more like self-justification than knowledge of self. Paradoxically, spectators find this final declaration quite the most absorbing part of the play. One would like to believe that this is not what the playwright intended !

KUMUD MEHTA

SILENCE ! THE COURT IS IN SESSION was first presented in English by the Madras players at the Museum Theatre, Madras in March 1971. It was directed by Ammu Mathew. The cast was as follows:

SAMANT	Viraf Kanga
BENARE	Vishalam Ekambaram
SUKHATME	S. Ramchander
SERVANT	V. Narayanam
BALU ROKDE	Nickoo
PONKSHE	P. C. Ramakrishna
KARNIK	Matthew Huntley
MRS KASHIKAR	Lakshmi Krishnamurty
MR KASHIKAR	S. V. Krishnamurty
LOCAL RESIDENT	Pradeep Singh Mehta

NOTE

I must express my thanks to Amol Palekar and Professor D. N. Govilkar for their help in checking respectively the language of the first and final drafts of the translation.

P. A.

ACT ONE

The lights go up on a completely empty hall. It has two doors. One to enter by, and one to go to an adjoining room. One side of the hall seems to go leftwards into the wings. Within the hall are a built-in platform, one or two old wooden chairs, an old box, a stool—and sundry other things lie jumbled together as if in a lumber-room. A clock, out of order, on the wall. Some worn-out portraits of national leaders. A wooden board with the names of donors. A picture of the god Ganesha, hung on the door. The door is closed.

There are footsteps outside. Someone unlocks the door. A man sidles in, and stands looking around as if seeing the hall for the first time. This is Samant. In his hands, a lock and key, a toy parrot made of green cloth, a book.

SAMANT [*looking around*]. This is it. Come in. This is the hall. They seem to have cleaned it up a bit this morning —because of the show. [*Miss Benare has entered after him, and is standing in the doorway. One fingertip is between her lips. She holds a basket of equipment, and a purse.*] What's the matter ? Did you catch your finger in the bolt ? These old bolts are all the same. They just won't slide straight. And if the bolt stays out just a little bit, and you don't pull it clean to one side, then what happens ? Shut the door—and you've had it ! Locked yourself in ! Suck it a little. You'll feel better. This finger of my right hand once got caught in the lock. For five days it was so swollen, I couldn't tell the difference between my finger and my thumb. I had to do *everything* with four fingers !

BENARE. Goodness ! [*to him*]. It's nothing. Nothing at all. It's just a habit with me. But I *am* feeling marvellous. I got down at the station with all the others, and suddenly, after many days, I felt wonderful !

SAMANT. Why's that ?

BENARE. Who knows ? And I felt even more wonderful coming here with you. I'm so glad the others fell behind !

We rushed ahead, didn't we ?

SAMANT. Yes, indeed. I mean to say, I'm not in the habit of walking so fast. You do set a very lively pace, very lively.

BENARE. Not always. But today, how I walked ! Let's leave everyone behind, I thought, and go somewhere far, far away—with you !

SAMANT [*in confusion*]. With me ?

BENARE. Yes, I like you very much.

SAMANT [*terribly shy and embarrassed*]. Tut-tut. Ha ha ! I'm hardly ...

BENARE. You're very nice indeed. And shall I tell you something ? You are a very pure and good person. I like you.

SAMANT [*incredulously*]. Me ?

BENARE. Yes, and I like this hall very much, too. [*She walks round it.*]

SAMANT. The hall too ? It's just an old one. Whenever there are functions in tne village, they take place here. You could say this hall just exists for the sake of functions. Speeches, receptions, weddings ... to say nothing of the women's *bhajan* group. They practise here in the afternoons. Tonight there's this programme, you see. So the *bhajan* practice must be off. They give *bhajans* a holiday when there's a show at night ! How else would the women finish their chores by nightfall ? Eh ?

BENARE [*cautious but inquisitive*]. Your wife is in the *bhajan* group, I suppose ?

SAMANT. Uh huh. Wrong. Not wife, sister-in-law. I don't have a wife at all.

BENARE [*pointing a finger at the green cloth parrot in his hand*]. Then who is *that* for ?

SAMANT. This, you mean ? For my nephew. A lovely child ! Do you like this toy ?

BENARE. Yes.

SAMANT. I'm not married yet. No particular reason. I earn enough to keep body and soul together. But I never got married. Do you know—there were magic shows here some time ago ? Sleight of hand, hypnotism and all that...

BENARE. Did you see them ?

SAMANT. What do you think! I'm here for every show.

BENARE. Is that so ?

SAMANT. Yes. I don't miss a single one. What other amusement is there in the village ?

BENARE. That's true. [*She goes very close to him, and says in confiding tones.*] Did you see the magic—from very near ?

SAMANT. Yes. That is, I wasn't *very* close. But still, close enough. Why ?

BENARE [*as close as ever*]. How do they do that—cutting a tongue, and putting it together again ?

SAMANT [*backing away a little*]. A tongue ? Tongue... well, it's hard to describe...

BENARE. But tell me ?

SAMANT. Eh ? But...

[*She comes as close as before. Embarrassed, he backs away once more.*]

It's like this ... I'll try ... I mean, I won't be able ... look, this is my tongue ...

[*He stretches the first joint of his finger towards her.*]

BENARE. Let me see.

[*She makes it an excuse to get even closer to him. For a moment or two, she is keenly aware of his nearness to her. But he is not.*]

SAMANT [*with concentration*]. This is my tongue. Look, it's cut ! Now what ? It'll bleed ! But it doesn't ? Why doesn't it bleed ? There must be something for it in hypnotism— that is, some trick. That's why it doesn't bleed. Nothing happens, nothing at all ... it doesn't even hurt—so ...

[*Perhaps as a response to his complete innocence, she moves away from him.*]

BENARE. Why haven't they reached here yet ? They always amble along. People should be brisk !

SAMANT. Yes. I was telling you about the tongue ... hypnotism—

BENARE. In school, when the first bell rings, my foot's already on the threshold. I haven't heard a single reproach for not being on time these past eight years. Nor about my teaching. I'm *never* behindhand with my lessons! Exercises corrected on time, too ! Not a bit of room for disapproval—I don't give an inch of it to any one !

SAMANT. You're a schoolmarm, it seems ?

BENARE. No, a teacher ! Do I seem the complete schoolmarm to you ?

SAMANT. No, no ... I didn't mean it like that ...

BENARE. Say it if you like ...

SAMANT. But I didn't say it at all ! A schoolmarm just means ... someone who—teaches—instructs !—children—that's what I meant to say ...

BENARE. They're so much better than adults. At least they don't have that blind pride of thinking they know everything. There's no nonsense stuffed in their heads. They don't scratch you till you bleed, then run away like cowards. Please open that window. It's become too hot for me. [*He opens the window eagerly. Benare takes a deep breath.*] Ah ! Now I feel better. No, no, I feel wonderful ! [*She starts walking freely round the hall once more.*]

SAMANT. Shall we finish that tongue trick now ? The hypnotism ? [*putting his finger out again.*] See that now. That's my tongue. Now it's cut.

BENARE. No! Not now.

SAMANT [*obediently*]. All right. [*He lowers his hand. Then suddenly comes forward, picking up a chair, and puts it down near her.*] Why are you wandering about ? Do sit down. Your feet will hurt.

BENARE. I'm used to standing while teaching. In class, I never sit when teaching. That's how I keep my eye on the whole class. No one has a chance to play up. My class is scared stiff of me ! And they adore me, too. My children will do anything for me. For I'd give the last drop of my blood to teach them. [*In a different tone*]. That's why people are jealous. Specially the other teachers and the management. But what can they do to me ? What can they do ? However hard they try, what *can* they do ? They're holding an enquiry, if you please ! But my teach-

ing's perfect. I've put my whole life into it—I've worn myself to a shadow in this job ! Just because of one bit of
slander, what can they do to me ? Throw me out ? Let
them ! I haven't hurt anyone. Anyone at all ! If I've
hurt anybody, it's been myself. But is that any kind of
reason for throwing me out ? Who are these people to say
what I can or can't do ? My life is my own—I haven't sold
it to anyone for a job ! My will is my own. My wishes are
my own. No one can kill those—no one ! I'll do what
I like with myself and my life ! I'll decide . . .
[*Unconsciously, her hand is on her stomach. She suddenly
stops. Seeing Samant, she falls silent. Gradually she regains
her poise. Samant is embarrassed.*]

SAMANT [*awkwardly*]. Shall I go and see why the others
haven't arrived yet ?

BENARE [*hastily*]. No. [*then coming back slowly to normal.*] I feel scared when I am alone, you know.

SAMANT. Then I won't go. Are you not feeling well ?

BENARE [*with a sudden access of energy*]. Nonsense ! Nothing's the matter with me. I'm fine. Just fine ! [*Clapping
her hands she starts crooning an English song to herself.*]

> Oh, I've got a sweetheart
> Who carries all my books,
> He plays in my doll house,
> And says he likes my looks.
> I'll tell you a secret—
> He wants to marry me.
> But Mummy says, I'm too little
> To have such thoughts as these.

[*She leaves off singing.*] Do you know what we are going
to do today, Mr—er—

SAMANT. Samant.

BENARE. Just so.

SAMANT. Yes. There's a notice by the temple. The Sonar
Moti Tenement (Bombay) Progressive Association's Mock
Law... law ... what was it ? Yes, Lawcourt ! At eight

sharp tonight.

BENARE. But what does that mean, do you think ?

SAMANT. That I don't know. Something to do with the court . . .

BENARE. Quite right. Not a real court; a fake one, a make-believe one !

SAMANT. In other words, some fun to do with a court.

BENARE. Exactly. Fun. But Samant, 'spreading enlighten-ment is also one of the Prime Objectives behind our pro-gramme'. So our chairman Kashikar will tell you. Kashi-kar can't take a step without a Prime Objective ! Besides him, there's Mrs Hand-that-Rocks-the-Cradle. I mean Mrs Kashikar. What an excellent housewife the poor woman is ! A real Hand-that-Rocks-the-Cradle type! But what's the use? Mr Prime Objective is tied up with uplifting the masses. And poor Hand-that-Rocks-the-Cradle has no cradle to rock !

SAMANT. You mean they have no—[*He rocks an imaginary baby in his arms.*]

BENARE. Right. You seem to be very bright, too ! Mr Kashikar and the Hand-that-Rocks-the-Cradle, in order that nothing should happen to either of them in their bare, bare house—and that they shouldn't die of boredom !—gave shelter to a young boy. They educated him. Made him toil away. Made a slave out of him. His name's Balu—Balu Rokde. Who else ? . . . Well, we have an Expert on the Law. He's such an- authority on the subject, even a desperate client won't go anywhere near him ! He just sits alone in the barristers' room at court, swatting flies with legal precedents! And in his tenement, he sits alone kil-ling houseflies ! But for today's mock trial. he's a very great barrister. You'll see the wonders he performs! And there's a 'Hmm !' with us ! (*Puts an imaginary pipe in her mouth.*) Hmm ! Sci-en-tist ! Inter-failed !

SAMANT. Oh, it does sound good fun!

BENARE. And we have an Intellectual too. That means someone who prides himself on his booklearning. But when there's a real-life problem, away he runs ! Hides his head.

He's not here today. Won't be coming, either. He wouldn't dare !

SAMANT. But what's today's trial about ?

BENARE. A case against President Johnson for producing atomic weapons.

SAMANT. Good heavens !

BENARE. Ssh ! I think they're here. [*She has an idea.*] Come here. Come on, hide like this. I'll stay here, too. Hide properly. Now ask them to come in.

[*Samant and Benare hiding behind the door that leads outside. Their bodies touch. Voices are heard saying, 'Here it is !' 'Found it at last !' as lawyer Sukhatme, science student Ponkshe and Balu Rokde, the Mock Lawcourt's general factotum, carrying between them two or three suitcases, two bags, a battery-operated microphone set, and the like, come in through the door. A lighted beedi in Sukhatme's mouth. A pipe between Ponkshe's lips. After them, a servant carrying two wooden enclosures—the dock and the witness-box. As they come in, Benare and Samant leap out from behind the door. She shouts 'Boo' in a tremendous voice. They all start for just a moment. Then one by one they recover their poise. Benare laughs to her heart's content. Samant stands looking around at all this, eagerly and wonderingly.*]

ROKDE [*going and setting down all his luggage at one spot*]. How loudly, Miss Benare ! All this might have fallen down! I would have been scolded by Mrs Kashikar. And all for nothing. Whatever happens, it's me she blames. I got a free education of them, didn't I ? So I'm paying for my sins !

[*The servant goes and puts the enclosures into the wings at left, and returns. Ponkshe pays him his porter's fees. Exit the servant.*]

PONKSHE [*weightily, removing his thick-framed spectacles*]. Oh, gosh ! Where is it ? ... [*He goes muttering into the inner room. to hunt for the lavatory.*]

SUKHATME [*inhaling deeply, and blowing out smoke*]. There is a little lassie, deep in my heart. Miss Benare, whatever happens, vou don't want to grow up, do you ? Eh ?

BENARE. Why, in the class room, I'm the soul of seriousness!

But I don't see why one should go around all the time with
a long face. Or a square face ! Like that Ponkshe ! We
should laugh, we should play, we should sing ! If we can
and if they'll let us, we should dance too. Shouldn't have
any false modesty or dignity. Or care for anyone ! I mean it.
When your life's over, do you think anyone will give you
a bit of theirs ? What do you say, Samant ? Do you think
they will ?

SAMANT. You're quite right. The great sage Tukaram said
... at least I *think* it was him—

BENARE. Forget about the sage Tukaram. I say it—I, Leela
Benare, a living woman, I say it from my own experience.
Life is not meant for anyone else. It's your own life. It
must be. It's a very, very important thing. Every moment,
every bit of it is precious—

SUKHATME [*clapping*].   Hear ! Hear !

[*Ponkshe comes out.*]

BENARE. Not here. [*She points to Ponkshe.*] There ! [*Tries
hard to control her laughter, but can't.*]

PONKSHE [*puzzled*].   What's the matter ?

BENARE. Ponkshe, tell the honest truth. Did you or did
you not go in looking for the 'arrangements' ? To deal
with your usual nervousness before a show ?

SUKHATME. Say what you will, Miss Benare. Our Ponkshe
looks most impressive during the trial. The scientist in the
witness-box ! A pipe and all that ! No one would believe
he has just taken his Inter-Science for the *second* time. Or
works as a clerk in the Central Telegraph Office !

[*Here Rokde, unable to control himself, laughs a little.*]

PONKSHE [*irritated*]. Don't you laugh, Rokde ! I didn't get
my education on Mrs Kashikar's charity ! I may have
failed my Inter-Science. But at least I did it on my own
father's money.   Nonsense !

BENARE. Nonsense ! [*She catches his exact intonation, and
laughs*]. Shall I tell you people something amusing ?
When I was small, I was very, very quiet. I just used to sit
and make plans—all by myself. I wouldn't tell anyone.
And at the slightest excuse, I used to cry loudly !

PONKSHE. In other words, the exact opposite of what you are now.

BENARE. Yes! Yes! Do you know, Samant—

SAMANT. [*promptly*]. Yes! That is, perhaps I don't... probably not, in fact...

BENARE. On the first day of school, I used to put nice fresh covers on every book I had. On the first page I used to write, in beautiful tiny letters, with pictures of flowers and things :

> The grass is green,
> The rose is red.
> This book is mine
> Till I am dead !

Till I am dead ! And do you know what happened ?

SAMANT. What happened ?

BENARE. Every single book got torn one by one and went I don't know where—but I am still here. I am not dead ! Not dead ! The grass is still green, the rose is still red, but I am not dead ! [*She starts laughing once more.*]

ROKDE. [*Quickly takes a notebook out of his bag and starts writing down the verse.*].

That's lovely ! The grass is—green. The—rose—is—red ... What was the rest of it, Miss Benare ?

BENARE [*the smile off her face*]. Rokde, this is a bad habit! I always tell the girls in class, don't be in a hurry to write down what you've hardly heard ! First listen ... say it to yourself slowly...send it deep inside you. Then it'll stay with you. It must mingle with your blood. It'll only stay once it's in your blood. No one can take it from you then—or make you forget it !

SAMANT. Our dear teacher used to say the same thing. He taught us verses by heart in just this way. This is, he didn't say all that about blood...

SUKHATME. Go on, Miss Benare.

BENARE [*suddenly expansive*]. Shall I tell you a story ? Children, be seated. There was once a wolf...

ROKDE [*suddenly sitting down cross-legged*]. Do tell it, miss.
Sit down, Mr Sukhatme. Ponkshe, sit down.
[*Ponkshe goes out with a look of annoyance on his face.*]
BENARE.   No. I'll recite a poem...

> Our feet tread on upon unknown
> And dangerous pathways evermore.
> Wave after blinded wave is shattered
> Stormily upon the shore.
> Light glows alive again.   Again
> It mingles with the dark of night.
> Our earthen hands burn out, and then
> Again in flames they are alight.
> Everything is fully known,
> And everything is clear to see.
> And the wound that's born to bleed
> Bleeds on for ever, faithfully.
> There is a battle sometimes, where
> Defeat is destined as the end.
> Some experiences are meant
> To taste, then just to waste and spend...*

[*leaving the poem in the middle*].   No—I'll sing a song.
'An old man from Malad came up to the fireside...An old
man from Malad, the old man's wife, the wife's little baby,
nurse, the nurse's visitor ...'
[*Sukhatme seated. Samant curious.* \As *Benare sings, for a
moment they all start beating the rhythm. Sukhatme claps
hands as if at a religious ceremony.   Enter the experimental
theatre actor, Karnik.   He is chewing* pan.]
KARNIK [*entering*].   Here we are.   I thought I had lost my
way.   [*He notices the others.*]   What's happened ?

---

* from a Marathi poem by Mrs Shirish Pai.
   Vijay Tendulkar, in the preface to the Marathi original of this
play, writes, 'The central character of Miss Benare came to me
through a poem. This beautiful poem by Mrs Shirish Pai has
been put into the first Act, in the lips of Miss Benare herself.'

ROKDE. Oh no ! That's spoilt everything !

SUKHATME. Benare was singing. [*In affected tones*]. Very nice. Very sweet, Miss Benare.

[*Benare sticks out her tongue at him to signify, 'I know what you mean!' and goes on laughing. Karnik is gazing round the hall. Rokde stands up.*].

SUKHATME [*in a flamboyant lawyer's voice*]. One minute, Mr Karnik! shall I tell you what's going through your mind right now ? This hall, you are thinking, is ideal for Intimate Theatre—in other words, for those plays of yours for a tiny audience. Which go over their heads in any case! Yes or not ? Answer me.

KARNIK [*on purpose, calmly chewing his* pan]. No. I was saying to myself, this hall would put even a real court to shame.

BENARE. *Goodness* ! That's wonderful! Our mock court tonight should go over well! Just like a real one!

ROKDE [*anxiously*]. But where's Mrs. Kashikar got to ?

KARNIK [*chewing his* pan]. She's on her way here. They stopped because Mr Kashikar wanted to buy a garland for her hair. So I bought my *pan*, and came ahead. Rokde, I hope the mike's batteries are all right. Test them now if you like. Or else you'll make a mess of it tonight! We must avoid last-minute disasters. But somehow they always happen. Last month, right in the middle of our show, a fuse blew ! I myself was on stage. So what if the role was a small one ? Somehow or other I managed to carry it off.

ROKDE. It was just an ordinary amateur play for the Ganapati Puja.

KARNIK. But the *mood* was destroyed!

BENARE [*yawns*; *then mischievously*]. Oh, it's not at what you were saying, Karnik. You see, I have to get up so early every day. There's the Morning Session, then the Afternoon Session. And on top of that, private tuition in the evening! I say, who's noticed something about Mr and Mrs Kashikar ?

ROKDE [*with instinctive, unconscious interest*]. What ?

PONKSHE [*re-entering*]. Yes, what ?

SUKHATME. I'll tell you. But no, I won't. You tell us yourself first, Miss Benare...eh ? Let me see...come on—out with it—

BENARE. You haven't understood a thing, Sukhatme. Don't give yourself those meaningless legal airs ! Well, although our Kashikar is a social worker and Mrs Kashikar is quite —er—quite uneducated and so on—of course, I don't think that education has any connection with a person's intelligence—well, although Mrs. Kashikar is not so educated, they are both so full of life ! I mean, Mr Kashikar buys garlands for Mrs Kashikar. Mrs Kashikar buys readymade bush-shirts for Mr Kashikar...It really makes one feel nice to see it !

[*Karnik opens a window backstage, spits* pan *juice through it, and comes downstage again.*]

KARNIK. When I for one see such public formalities between husband and wife, I suspect something quite different in private.

ROKDE [*rather angrily*]. That's the effect of modern theatre !

KARNIK. Don't meddle in what you don't understand, Rokde. You're still a child. Just stick to your college work. For my part, I never buy garlands for my wife. Even if I feel like it, I suppress the idea.

[*Benare tut-tuts audibly.*]

What's the matter ?

BENARE. If I were in your place, I would buy one for her daily!

SUKHATME. Then hurry up and start buying bush-shirts for your husband, Miss Benare ! I wonder what that most fortunate man will be like! If he's half as mischievous as you are, you've both had it !

BENARE. Never mind about that. [*suddenly looking around, to Samant*] Couldn't we please have some chairs here, Mr— What's-your-name—

SAMANT. Chairs ? Oh, my name's Samant, I mean ! [*Gets up and looks here and there*]. I'll have a look. How should I know...[*Exits, hunting.*]

PONKSHE. They're inside. Folding chairs. I could do with

some tea.

SUKHATME. When we had some at the station, you said no. [*'So now do without,' says his tone.*]

PONKSHE. Gosh, I didn't want it then. I don't agree with the way you people plan everything in advance. Call that living ? In this scientific age, it's fun to get everything at the last minute, without effort. [*Snaps his fingers.*] Like that!

[*Just then, Samant enters from the inner room, and stands in the doorway, both arms full of as many folding chairs as he can carry.*]

SAMANT [*putting them down in the hall*]. There are more if you want. Inside. [*All of them snappily open the chairs and sit down wherever they can. Conversation. Ponkshe still standing showing off his pipe*].

SAMANT [*to Ponkshe, awed by his sahib-like appearance*]. Do sit down, sahib.

PONKSHE [*pleased at the 'sahib'*]. No, thank you. I was sitting in the train Er—what's your name ?

SAMANT. Samant. I'm from this village, sir.

PONKSHE. Good ! Can we have some tea here ?

SAMANT. Tea ? Yes, sir. But sugar will be the problem. You can't get sugar these days. If *gur* will do—

PONKSHE. No. You probably don't know, Mr. Samant. *Gur* in tea is poisonous.

SAMANT. But at our house, that's what we grown-ups usually take. Normally the sugar ration isn't even enough for my brother's children. They just can't drink tea without sugar. So what can we do ?

PONKSHE [*pipe in mouth, most scientist-like*]. Hmm !

BENARE [*unable to resist teasing him, mimics him from where she is sitting*]. Hmm. Once there was a Hmm ! And he knew a girl called Erhmm !

PONKSHE. Stop it, Benare ! Don't be childish. [*Samant still standing. Mr and Mrs Kashikar enter.*]

MRS KASHIKAR [*unconsciously stroking the garland in her hair*]. Look, here they all are, after all !

SUKHATME. Come in, Kashikar ! How did the garland-buying go ?

[*Benare is pointing them out to Samant with gestures.*]

ROKDE [*coming forward*]. Yes, how did it ?

MRS KASHIKAR. Balu, have you brought all the luggage ?

ROKDE. Absolutely.

KASHIKAR. Each time you say you've brought it all, Rokde, and each time you forget something. Have you got the usher's staff ? Don't just nod your head. Show it if you have it. Let me see.

ROKDE [*producing it*]. Here it is. (*Pathetically*) I've got the uniform too. I only forget things sometimes. Not all the time.

KASHIKAR. I don't care if you always forget. At least today I hope everything's in order. Or you'll make a mess of things. My judge's wig ? Did you bring it ?

ROKDE. Yes. I brought that first. [*Rokde grows increasingly miserable and irritated.*]

KASHIKAR. You, Sukhatme ? Did you bring your lawyer's gown ?

SUKHATME [*bowing as if in court*]. Yes, milord ! I don't forget that even in my dreams ! What about you, Ponkshe ?

PONKSHE. Well, I come fully dressed, so I won't forget a thing. I have this nervous temperament a bit, you know. If I don't have my pipe, I can't remember a thing in the witness-box.

MRS KASHIKAR. I'll rehearse your lines with you a little, before today's show.

PONKSHE. No need for that.

MRS KASHIKAR. I say, Benare—(*stroking the garland in her hair*) I did mean to buy a garland for you too—

BENARE [*in Ponkshe's tones*]. Hmm !

[*Ponkshe bites his lips angrily.*]

MRS KASHIKAR [*to Mr Kashikar*]. Didn't I, dear ? But what happened was that—

BENARE [*laughing heartily*].—The garland flew away—pouf ! Or did the dicky-bird take it ? I never want garlands. If I did, couldn't I afford to buy them ? I earn my own living, you know. That's why I never feel like buying garlands and things.

[*Benare hands out the snacks Mrs Kashikar has brought.*]

MRS KASHIKAR. Well, what does your school have to say for itself ?

BENARE [*carefully*]. My school says nothing.

KASHIKAR. I wonder, should we have the judge's chair this side or that ?

KARNIK. Here, of course. The entrance is over there. That room next door can be used for the judge. You can enter from there. President Johnson will stand over here like this—

SAMANT [*amazed*]. President Johnson !

KASHIKAR. No, no. Johnson's dock should be left over there. So when I speak as the judge—

KARNIK. I don't agree. If you look at it from the audience's point of view, it should be right here—

SUKHATME. Mr Karnik, I shall prosecute you for seeing things from the audience's point of view ! And you a man of the modern theatre ! [*A lawyer's laugh.*]

KARNIK. Yet again ! Will someone please tell me what this Modern Theatre is supposed to be ? People just play with words without knowing what they mean. I do what seems right to me. Whether it's modern or old-fashioned doesn't matter. [*They begin to argue.*]

SAMANT [*stopping Rokde*]. What's this business about President Johnson ?

ROKDE [*Deep in his own thoughts, starts*]. Who ?

SAMANT. They said 'President Johnson' or something just now.

ROKDE. Oh, that !

SAMANT. Do you mean President Johnson will really—probably he won't, however—I mean, what's it all about ?

ROKDE. Not the real one ! This fellow Karnik here plays him ! [*He is getting his revenge on Karnik for putting him in his place earlier.*]

SAMANT. President Johnson !

ROKDE [*Suddenly remembering, comes and stops Mrs Kashikar*]. Madam, Professor Damle hasn't arrived yet !

[*Benare, who had been talking to Mrs Kashikar, suddenly falls silent and motionless. Then she goes by mistake to Ponkshe, and stands talking to him, with an artificial air. He is silent.*]

MRS KASHIKAR. Well, he'll come late as usual. He told me on the phone that he wouldn't be able to catch our train. He was doing a symposium—or something—in the university. I've told him about this twice. Benare, did you meet him ?

BENARE [*who is talking to Ponkshe*]. Whom ?

MRS KASHIKAR. Professor Damle.

BENARE. No, I didn't.

[*Starts talking to Ponkshe again. He is silent. No response at all.*]

ROKDE [*after consulting Samant, to Mrs Kashikar*]. But madam, Samant here says that the next train doesn't reach here till nine p.m. How will that do? It'll be too late!

PONKSHE [*in the gap in the conversation*]. What happened afterwards to that friend of yours, Miss Benare ? That girl—the one in trouble—whom you found for me to marry . . .

[*Benare confused. In her confusion she goes to Samant.*]

MRS KASHIKAR. There was a train in between, wasn't there? [*to Kashikar*] Dear, Balu here says there's no train in between—

KASHIKAR [*interrupting his argument with Karnik.*] In between what ?

ROKDE [*to him*]. Samant here says there's no train now before the show !

SUKHATME. There's one afterwards, isn't there ? That's good enough !

KASHIKAR. But my dear Sukhatme, how will Professor Damle get here ? He'll arrive late. If he comes at all ! There's no train in between.

KARNIK. Then he won't come at all, I'm telling you. Professor Damle is quite calculating, that way. When you talk of being late, he just cancels the programme, and sits comfortably at home.

ROKDE [*tense*]. Madam, I did drop a postcard to him as usual—when I sent one to all the others—I mean, it's no fault of mine—I even wrote the address right—

KASHIKAR. Here's a hitch !

SUKHATME. What's so serious about it ? Don't worry in the least !

KASHIKAR. How can I not worry ? We owe something to the people, Sukhatme. A performance is no laughing matter.

PONKSHE [*coming up*]. What's happened ?

MRS KASHIKAR [*to Sukhatme*]. But now who'll play the counsel for the accused ?

SUKHATME. Don't you worry. For today, I'll do that role along with that of the prosecuting counsel. What's so serious about that ? I'm a lawyer to the marrow ! I tell you, Kashikar, just leave it to me.

KARNIK. Yes, I think that will be much more dramatic !

PONKSHE. Definitely ! [*A pompous puff at his pipe.*]

BENARE. Definitely !

[*Ponkshe looks at her angrily.*]

ROKDE [*consulting a paper he is holding*]. And the fourth witness. Mr Sukhatme, he's missing, too. Rawte is sick with flu. We'd decided to take a local man. [*He catches sight of Mrs Kashikar, and corrects himself.*] That is, *you* had decided . . .

SUKHATME. True. A local man—that means . . .

ROKDE [*gathering up his courage*]. Can I please do that part today ? It's just a small one—anyone can do mine—I know the fourth witness's lines off by heart . . .

KARNIK. I oppose it ! Even if you're just an usher, your character isn't an easy one to play. So what if he has no lines ? It can't be managed by putting up someone else at the last minute. Stick to your part, Rokde.

ROKDE. But how does it matter if just one day I play another role ?

KASHIKAR. No.

MRS KASHIKAR. Balu, if he says no, then don't do it !

2

[*Rokde falls back.*] But then, who will be the fourth witness ?

SUKHATME [*staring at Samant*]. I—know ! [*suddenly*] Here's your fourth witness—[*points to him*] Samant !

SAMANT [*starting*]. What's the matter ?

PONKSHE [*puffing at his pipe*]. Not bad !

KASHIKAR [*to Samant*]. Have you ever acted in a play ?

SAMANT. Good heavens, no ! Never at all. What's the matter ?

MRS KASHIKAR. Will you be the fourth witness ? Look here, Benare. [*She comes over.*] What do you think of this gentleman as the fourth witness ?

BENARE. This gentleman ? Not bad—I think he's lovely ! [*Samant embarrassed. Benare smiling.*] As a witness, I mean. The fourth witness.

SUKHATME. Mrs Kashikar, Karnik, Ponkshe, don't worry ! I'll take the responsibility. Nothing to it ! I'll prepare him. Mister—what's your name ?—

SAMANT. Raghu Samant.

SUKHATME. Mr Samant, you have been called as fourth witness for today's Living Lawcourt.

SAMANT [*flabbergasted and trembling*]. But I honestly don't know anything about it !

MRS KASHIKAR. You've seen a court, haven't you ?

SAMANT. Never in my life !

KARNIK. In a play, at least ?

SAMANT. No. Not at all ! No play like that has ever been seen here.

SUKHATME [*taunting Karnik*]. It's a good thing, he hasn't seen a courtroom in a play. At least he won't have all kinds of wrong notions about it !

KARNIK. Confine your remarks to *certain* plays !

SUKHATME. Mr Samant, I'll have you word-perfect before the show. After all, you don't have to teach a lawyer how to coach witnesses ! [*He gives a lawyer's laugh.*]

SAMANT. But I'm not used to it at all ! The very thought that it's a court will terrify me !

MRS KASHIKAR. I suggest we have a rehearsal with him. [*to

Mr Kashikar] What do you think, dear ? [*He pays no attention, so*] What do you think, Benare ?

BENARE. Yes. I've no objection at all. I was wondering what
to do till the show. I forgot to bring a book to read.

SAMANT. Oh. Would you like the new novel by Suryakant
Phatarphekar ? I've just got it. [*Fishes it out and proffers
it.*] His novels are so thrilling ! This is the 105th.

BENARE. Then I certainly don't want it !

SUKHATME. Well, we have the Bible and the Bhagavad-
Geeta for the oath-taking—I mention it because you want
something to read. By the way, Rokde, you did bring
along the Bible and the Geeta, didn't you ? Or have you
forgotten ?

ROKDE [*in an agonized voice*]. No, they're here. I'll show
them to you if you want.

[*Goes towards the bags. But doesn't show the Geeta.*]

BENARE. Learned Counsel, I'm not yet so old as to be reading
those books !

KASHIKAR. Then you must be reading *True Stories* or maga-
zines like that. That's what my wife reads. Quite amusing,
they are. Because of my social work, I can't manage to
do more than look at the pictures.

MRS KASHIKAR [*protesting*]. Really !

KASHIKAR [*annoyed*]. What do you mean, 'Really' ! Wasn't
I speaking the truth ?

[*Mrs Kashikar's face falls.*]

KARNIK. I think the idea of a rehearsal is excellent. If only
someone would fetch four or five packets of cigarettes.
That's all we need, so we won't have to go out in the
middle.

PONKSHE. I don't mind. [*Puffing at his pipe.*]

SAMANT [*to Rokde*]. Then it doesn't matter. If I see it all
once, there's no question about it. That'll reassure me. Eh ?
[*Rokde doesn't answer.*]

BENARE. Shall I tell you something ? We've done tonight's
atomic weapons trial seven times in the past three months.
Tonight's the eighth time. I've no objection to doing it
once more before that. But I do think tonight's proper

show will fall flat.

SUKHATME. I agree with Miss Benare. I have an idea. See if you like it. When we lawyers are at ease in the barristers' room, we sometimes play rummy. Or patience. Or a certain other game. Just to pass the time, that's all. You bring a new and imaginary case against someone. Eh ? Shall we do that? Let's have an imaginary case. So Samant here will understand how a court works. And we'll pass the time more pleasantly. What do you say, Mr Kashikar ? Do we have your sanction ?

KASHIKAR. That's all right. It doesn't do for a man in public life to show too much hesitation. One must act according to the majority's wishes.

KARNIK [excited]. Three cheers for this new idea ! In Drama Theory we call this a Visual Enactment. I heard of it at the Government Drama Camp last year.

SUKHATME. Why give such a hard name to a simple thing ? This is just a game. Eh, Miss Benare ?

BENARE. I'm even willing to play hopscotch, if you're talking of games. Games are very good for you. I often play quite happily with the children at school. It's fun.

PONKSHE. All right, we'll play. Mr Samant, could you please fetch some packets of cigarettes from the corner ? Capstans for me. Here you are. [Gives him money.]

MRS KASHIKAR. Why are you paying, Ponkshe ? Samant, give it back. What I say is, let's call it Performance Expenses—that'll be all right. In any case, we have to demonstrate our lawcourt to Samant because of the performance, don't we ? That settles it. Samant, [opening her purse, and taking out a banknote] take this. Bring half a dozen packets of the kind everyone wants. And bring some pan, three or four. Sweet ones.

SAMANT. Yes. [Goes out with the money. Coming back] Don't start, will you ? I'll be back in a minute. [Exit.]

BENARE. Poor thing ! I'll be back.

[Takes a face towel and a cake of soap out of her basket. Goes inside humming to herself.]

MRS KASHIKAR. Balu, start arranging the court.

[*He sets to work.*]

KARNIK. Ponkshe, come here a minute. [*To Sukhatme and the others*] The same cast as tonight ? In other words, the same judge, counsel etc. ?

SUKHATME. Oh yes. By all means. Why change it ? I'll play the lawyers.

MRS KASHIKAR. But what I say is, let the accused at least be different. What do you think, Karnik ?

KARNIK. No. It's not necessary. [*Aside to Ponkshe, who has reached him*] Do you know something, Ponkshe ?

PONKSHE. What ?

KARNIK [*indicating the inner room*]. About her ? About Miss Benare. Rokde told me.

PONKSHE. What ?

KARNIK. Not now. Remind me tonight. After the show.

PONKSHE. I've got something to tell you, too. About Miss Benare. [*To the others*] If you ask me, it's a good idea. A different prisoner.

KASHIKAR. It'll add that bit of variety, I would say.

MRS KASHIKAR. Exactly.

KASHIKAR. What do you mean, exactly ? Hold your tongue. Can't say a word ! . . .

[*Mrs Kashikar is silenced.*]

SUKHATME. I don't mind. The accused—I feel—why not Rokde ? [*Rokde is delighted.*]

ROKDE. Yes, indeed. I'm ready to—

PONKSHE. No! (*To Karnik*) I also have something to tell you—about her !

KARNIK. I'll be the accused.

KASHIKAR. I suggest that if we are going through with it, it should not be a frivolous, facetious affair ! I'll be the accused, Sukhatme. Make me the accused.

KARNIK. What importance for him ! He'll be the judge, he'll be the accused !

PONKSHE [*puffing at his pipe*]. Consider me, then ! I'm not keen, as such, you know. But if I'll do, I'm game.

ROKDE [*to Mrs Kashikar*]. But what's wrong with me, madam ?

MRS KASHIKAR. Shall I do it ? I will if you like.

KASHIKAR. No !

[*Mrs Kashikar falls silent.*]

She can't get among a few people without wanting to show off ! Shows off all the time !

MRS KASHIKAR [*quite put out.*] Enough. I won't do it ! Satisfied ? [*She is thoroughly disheartened.*]

SUKHATME. We don't need to take any of you. Kashikar, let's have a really different kind of accused. Eh ? Let's have our Miss Benare ! Eh, Ponkshe ? What d'you think of my choice ?

PONKSHE. It's good.

SUKHATME. Then where's the need for argument ? Well, Mrs Kashikar ?

MRS KASHIKAR. If you say so, it's all right. In any case, we'll be able to see what the trial of a woman is like. [*Out of sheer habit, to Mr Kashikar*] Isn't that so, dear ? One should have that experience—

KASHIKAR [*sarcastically*]. Of course ! I suppose they're just about to make you a judge of the Supreme Court !—

MRS KASHIKAR. That's not how I meant it . . .

SUKHATME. There's not much difference between one trial and another. But when there's a woman in the dock, the case does have a different complexion, that's true. That is my experience. Well, Mr Karnik ?

KARNIK. It's all right. I won't stay outside the team. I believe in team spirit.

MRS KASHIKAR. Then it's settled. Our accused for now is Benare. But what's the charge ?

KASHIKAR. It should be a charge with social significance.

PONKSHE. All right. [*Gets up.*] Sh ! Shall we do something ? Come to me, all of you. Come on. Come here.

[*Whispers some plan to them, gesticulating. Every now and then, he points to the room where Benare is.*]

KASHIKAR. Rokde, haven't you finished arranging the court yet ?

ROKDE. I've finished. [*Bustles about, showing haste.*]

KARNIK. That's why I drew you a ground plan, Rokde. To

show which properties go where.

ROKDE [*angrily*]. I don't understand your theatrical matters.
I'm not used to them.

[*All of them arrange the furniture as in court, Ponkshe taking the lead. Kashikar supervises. On Ponkshe's instruc-
tions Rokde picks up Benare's purse from the luggage on
the dais, and places it on a stool at left. The furniture ar-
rangement is completed. Ponkshe and Kashikar go and
stand by the door of the inner room. All the others go into the wings at the left.*]

KASHIKAR [*to the people going into the wings*]. I'll give
you a signal.

[*Now Benare comes out singing, wiping her face on the
towel. She looks very fresh.*]

BENARE [*singing while she puts away the napkin, soap etc.
in the basket on the dais at right.*]

       The parrot to the sparrow said,
       'Why, oh why are your eyes so red ?'
       'Oh, my dear friend, what shall I say ?
       Someone has stolen my nest away.'
       Sparrow, sparrow, poor little sparrow !

PONKSHE [*coming from the doorway of the inner room
and standing before Miss Benare on the dais*]. Miss Leela
Benare, you have been arrested on suspicion of a crime of
an extremely grave nature, and brought as a prisoner before the bar of this court.

[*She stiffens where she is. She looks around her numbly. He
is gazing at her. She goes towards the wings at left, looking for her purse, to put the comb in her hands away.
Picks up the purse from the stool. Meanwhile, Kashikar
comes and seats himself on the judge's chair on the dais.
He signals to the people in the wings. Karnik and Rokde
silently bring the wooden dock and arrange it around Benare. Sukhatme comes from the wings putting on his black
lawyer's gown, and sits in a chair next to the broken-
down lawyer's table. The others go to their places. Samant
enters and stands in the doorway.*]

KASHIKAR [*clearing his throat*]. Prisoner Miss Benare, under

Section No. 302 of the Indian Penal Code you are accused of the crime of infanticide. Are you guilty of the aforementioned crime ?

[*Benare looks stunned. All are silent for the moment. The atmosphere is extraordinarily sombre.*]

CURTAIN

ACT TWO

The same hall. The situation is the same as at the end of Act One.

KASHIKAR [*sitting at the table with the dignity of a judge*]. Prisoner Miss Benare, under Section No. 302 of the Indian Penal Code, you have been accused of the crime of infanticide. Are you guilty or not guilty of the aforementioned crime ?

[*The atmosphere is extraordinarily sombre. Miss Benare stands numbly with a chair for support.*]

SAMANT [*still standing in the doorway, says softly to Karnik.*] Here they are. *Màsala pan* and cigarettes.

[*At this, the atmosphere at once lightens.*]

MRS KASHIKAR. A sweet one for me.

KARNIK. A packet of Wills for me.

PONKSHE. Samant, one special *pan* here.

SUKHATME. One *pan*, one packet of *beedis*. What about you, Kashikar ?

KASHIKAR. A *masala pan*.

[*Rokde takes the* pan *from Samant and brings it over to Kashikar.*]

ROKDE [*with great politeness, to Kashikar*]. I've taken the astringent out of it.

SUKHATME [*offering a* pan *to Benare*]. Here, have one, Miss Benare.

BENARE [*who is sitting on the chair*]. What ? Yes—I mean no. Thank you.

SUKHATME. Why are you so grave all of a sudden ? After all, it's a game. Just a game, that's all. Why are you so serious ?

BENARE [*trying to laugh*]. Who's serious ? I'm absolutely —lighthearted. I just got a bit serious to create the right atmosphere. For the court, that's all. Why should I be afraid of a trial like this ?

SAMANT [*lighting a cigarette Karnik has given him, to Karnik*]. It seems there was some joke just now ?

KARNIK [*inhaling*]. What joke ?

SAMANT. No, he made some accusation—Mr Kashikar ...
but I didn't quite catch it.

KARNIK. The charge ? Infanticide.

SAMANT. That's right. But what's that ? I just don't understand, that's why I ask...I'm just an ignorant person.

SUKHATME. The crime of killing a new-born child.

SAMANT. Good heavens ! A terrible charge ! That's exactly
what happened in our village—it must be one or two years
ago now—the poor woman was a widow.

SUKHATME. Is that so ? Who was the lawyer on the case ?
Kashikar, you've really picked some charge ! A first-class
charge ! There's no fun in a case unless there's a really
thundering charge !

KASHIKAR. Did you notice, also, Sukhatme, that this charge
is important from the social point of view ? The question
of infanticide is one of great social significance. That's
why I deliberately picked it. We consider society's best
interests in all we do. Come on, Miss Benare. Rokde, my
gavel.

[Rokde brings over the gavel fussily.]

It wouldn't have mattered, if I didn't have it just now. I
was checking whether you'd brought it. [Banging the ga-
vel] Now to business. Come on, come on, Sukhatme.
Make a start. *Adhikasya adhikam phalam.* 'Best efforts
bring best results.' First my earpick ... [Searches for it in
his pocket, and places it by him.]

SUKHATME [moving his lawyer's gown about with an important air, and chewing pan]. Milord, in the interests of the
smooth functioning of the matter before this court, I be-
seech the court for an adjournment of a quarter minute
at the beginning, so that all present may spit out the *pan*
in their mouths.

KASHIKAR [spitting out bits of pan with all the dignity of a
judge]. Counsel for the accused should present his plea
in the matter.

SUKHATME [immediately rising, and becoming the counsel
for the accused]. Milord, I strictly oppose the suggestion
of my learned friend, the counsel for the prosecution. Whe-

reas ten seconds are enough to spit out *pan,* my learned
friend is asking for a quarter minute. It is clear that my
learned friend has an aim of wasting time, which is inju-
rious and troublesome to my client. Therefore we move
that an adjournment of ten seconds only be granted.

BENARE [*unable to restrain herself*]. Yes. Or else no—only
nine-and-a-half seconds.

KASHIKAR. Miss Benare, the accused is not supposed to interrupt the court. It's one thing for Samant. But should
I have to explain the court's etiquette to you afresh ?
[*Gravely summoning Karnik*] Clerk of the court, please
bring to the attention of this court the legal precedent
concerning the matter which has been moved before us.

KARNIK [*removing the cigarette from his mouth, and blowing out a great deal of smoke*]. Considering that it has not
been the normal practice in court to conduct a case while
chewing *pan,* I do not think any precedent has been estab-
lished in this matter. Moreover, this instance of a judge's
chewing *pan* in court is the first one, and so somewhat
unprecedented, Milord.

KASHIKAR. Counsel for the defence, are you able to establish before the court that it is possible to spit out *pan* in
ten seconds ?

SUKHATME. By all means. [*Goes outside, spits, and shut-
ting the door*] Exactly ten seconds, Milord.

KASHIKAR. We must see for ourselves. [*Rising, goes inside
to do just that.*]

BENARE [*sighing*]. Is this a court of law, Karnik, or a spitting contest ?

[*Karnik pays no attention.*]

SAMANT [*after a moment, to Karnik*]. Sir, does a real court
truly work like this ? It's very interesting.

KARNIK [*blowing out cigarette smoke, with mock seriousness*]. Ssh. You'll commit contempt of court. Just listen.
[*Winks at Ponkshe.*]

KASHIKAR [*coming back and sitting down*]. Clerk of the
court, how long did that take ?

KARNIK [*looking at his watch*]. Who knows ?

MRS KASHIKAR. I'll tell you It was fifteen seconds.

SUKHATME [*As the counsel for the prosecution, with a triumphant laugh*]. There ! Not ten, but a full fifteen seconds—that is, a quarter minute. A quarter minute ! Exactly the time I told you, Milord.

KASHIKAR [*maintaining his grave manner throughout*]. Yes. Now, seeing that more than half a minute of the court's time has been wasted in this research and experimentation on the subject of spitting *pan*, it is this court's serious decision that the matter before it should proceed without further delay. So long as it is done individually by you, and is inoffensive to the court, everyone may of course spit *pan*.

PONKSHE [*rising*]. Hear, hear !

KASHIKAR [*banging his gavel*]. Silence ! Silence must be observed.

MRS KASHIKAR [*to Samant*]. Samant, all this about *pan* and and so on is just in fun, you know. Just notice the practice in court. The important thing is, you need the court's permission for everything. Or you'll make a mistake tonight.

SAMANT [*excitedly*]. No. Of course, I'm watching. But—

KASHIKAR [*banging the gavel*]. Silence must be observed while the court is in session. Can't shut up at home, can't shut up here !

MRS KASHIKAR. But I was just telling Samant here—

SUKHATME. Let it pass, Mrs Kashikar. He's just joking.

MRS KASHIKAR. So what ? Scolding me at every step !

BENARE [*a little worried, to Rokde, who is playing the usher*]. I say, Balu . . .

ROKDE [*angry but controlling his voice*]. Don't call me Balu !

KASHIKAR [*clearing his throat, and banging the gavel*]. Now, back to infanticide. Prisoner Miss Leela Benare, are you guilty or not guilty of the charge that has been brought against you ?

BENARE. Would *you* admit yourself guilty of it ?

KASHIKAR [*banging the gavel*]. Order, order ! The dignity of the court must be preserved at all costs. Or Samant will not grasp how a court really works.

BENARE. Or how infanticide really works ? Really, I don't like your word at all ! Infanticide...infanticide ! Why don't you accuse me instead of—um—snatching public property ! That has a nice sound about it, don't you think ? Sounds like 'snatching' !

MRS KASHIKAR. I don't think so at all. There's nothing wrong with the present charge.

BENARE [*banging her hand on the chair*]. Order, order ! The dignity of the court must be preserved at all costs. Can't shut up at home, can't shut up here ! [*Imitating a lawyer*] Milord, let the court's family be given a suitable reprimand. She has never committed the crime of infanticide. Or stolen any public property except for Milord himself !

MRS KASHIKAR. That's enough, Benare !

BENARE [*softly, to the usher Rokde*]. I say, Balu--[*He bites his lips angrily.*]

SAMANT [*enthusiastically, to Mrs Kashikar*]. Ha ha ! Miss Benare is really amazing !

PONKSHE [*seriously*] In many respects.

KASHIKAR. Prisoner Miss Benare, for abrogating the authority of counsel, and for obstructing the due process of the law, a reprimand is hereby issued to you.

BENARE [*getting up from her seat, and coming up to him and offering him the pan near him*]. Thanks ! For that, a *masala pan* is hereby issued to you.

KARNIK. This is it ! This is what I meant ! If nothing is going to be taken seriously at all, there's the end of the matter. Miss Benare, at least so that Samant can understand something, please obey the rules of the court. Be serious !

SUKHATME. Otherwise, this game becomes really childish. We need seriousness.

BENARE [*coming back to her place*]. Now, back to infanticide. I was wrong, Milord. But there's no reason for the prisoner to show such respect for the judge. I plead not

guilty. I couldn't even kill a common cockroach. I'm scared to do it. How could I kill a newborn child ? I know
I got annoyed this morning in my class at school. And
gave a naughty pupil a good whack ! So what ? What
can one do ? The brats won't listen to you.

KASHIKAR. Rokde, the book for the oath-taking ?

[Rokde hurriedly takes out a fat volume, places it on the
stool nearby.]

The witness-box ?

[Rokde goes to fetch it.]

MRS KASHIKAR [to Samant]. After this, there's the prosecution's speech.

SUKHATME [who is sitting with his feet stretched across
another chair, and his hands clasped behind his head, gets
up lazily. Mechanically, he says]. Milord, the nature of
the charge brought against the accused (lights up his
beedi from Karnik's cigarette, and breathes out smoke)
is a most terrible one. Motherhood is a sacred thing—

BENARE. How do you know ? [seeing everyone's expres-
sions] Order, order !

[Ponkshe, fed up, goes into the inner room.]

KASHIKAR. Prisoner Miss Benare, for obstructing the work
of the court, a second reprimand is hereby issued to you.
Counsel for the prosecution, continue.

SUKHATME. Motherhood is pure. Moreover, there is a great
—er—a great nobility in our concept of motherhood. We
have acknowledged woman as the mother of mankind.
Our culture enjoins us to perpetual worship of her. 'Be
thy mother as a god' is what we teach our children from
infancy. There is great responsibility devolving upon a
mother. She weaves a magic circle with her whole existence
in order to protect and preserve her little one—

KASHIKAR. You've forgotten one thing. There's a Sanskrit
proverb. *Janani janmabhumishcha svargadapi gariyasi.*

> 'Mother and
> The Motherland,
> Both are even
> Higher than heaven.'

MRS KASHIKAR [*with enthusiasm*]. And of course, 'Great are thy favours, O mother' is quite famous.

BENARE. Order, order ! This is all straight out of a school composition-book. [*Bites her tongue ironically.*] Prisoner Miss Benare, for abrogating the authority of the court, a reprimand is *once more* issued to you ! [*Pretends to bang a gavel.*]

SUKHATME. I am deeply grateful, Milord, for your addition. In short, 'Woman is a wife for a moment, but a mother for ever.'

[*Samant claps.*]

MRS KASHIKAR. It's all right now, but you mustn't do that tonight, you know.

SAMANT. All right. I just couldn't help it. What a sentence, eh ?

SUKHATME. It is true. Considering this, what would we respectable citizens say if any woman were to take the life of the delicate bundle of joy she has borne ? We would say, there could be no baser or more devilish thing on earth. I intend to establish by means of evidence that the prisoner has done this same vile deed.

[*Rokde brings the witness-box.*]

BENARE [*softly and mischievously, to Rokde*]. I say, Balu— [*He is thoroughly annoyed. Ponkshe comes out of the inner room.*]

SUKHATME. My first witness is the world-famous scientist, Mr Gopal Ponkshe. Well, Ponkshe ? Are you happy ? I've suddenly promoted you to world fame, eh ?

KASHIKAR. Call the witness to the witness-box. [*He is picking his ear.*]

[*Ponkshe enters the witness-box. Rokde holds the big volume in front of him.*]

PONKSHE [*glancing at the first page of the volume, and placing his hand on it, says gravely*]. I, G. N. Ponkshe, placing my hand upon the Oxford English Dictionary, do hereby solemnly swear that I shall tell the truth, the whole truth, and nothing but the truth.

[*Benare laughs and laughs.*]

MRS KASHIKAR [*in intimidating tones*]. Balu, where is the Geeta ?

ROKDE. [*miserably*]. I forgot it. I brought the Dictionary by mistake. [*grumbling*] How much can I possibly remember ?

BENARE. Poor Balu !

ROKDE. Don't pity me, I'm warning you !

KASHIKAR [*banging his gavel*]. Begin the examination !

MRS KASHIKAR [*to Samant, in a conspiratorial whisper*]. Just observe this examination. All right ?

[*Samant nods his head.*]

SUKHATME [*approaching Ponkshe*]. Your name ?

PONKSHE. G. N. Ponkshe. Go further on. We can have all the details tonight.

SUKHATME. Mr Ponkshe, are you acquainted with the accused ?

BENARE [*suddenly, in Ponkshe's manner*]. Hmm !

PONKSHE [*looking carefully at Benare*]. Yes. Very well indeed.

SUKHATME. How would you describe her social status ?

PONKSHE. A teacher. In other words, a schoolmarm.

BENARE [*sticking her tongue out at him*]. But I'm still quite young !

SUKHATME. Mr Ponkshe, is the accused married or unmarried ?

PONKSHE. Why don't you ask the accused ?

SUKHATME. But if you were asked, what would you say ?

PONKSHE. To the public eye, she is unmarried.

BENARE [*interrupting*]. And to the private eye ?

KASHIKAR. Order ! Miss Benare, self-control. Don't forget the value of self-control. [*to Sukhatme*] You may continue. I'll just be back. [*Rises and goes to the inner room, where the toilet is.*]

MRS KASHIKAR. All this is all right for now, you know. It won't be like this at night. That'll have to be done properly.

SUKHATME [*to himself*]. The wrong things always seem to happen to Mr Kashikar at the wrong time... (*aloud*) Mr Ponkshe, how would you describe your view of the moral conduct of the accused ? On the whole like that of a normal unmarried woman ? You at least should take this trial seriously.

BENARE. But how should he know what the moral conduct of a normal unmarried woman is like ?

PONKSHE [*paying no attention to her*]. It is different.

SUKHATME. For example ?

PONKSHE. The accused is a bit too much.

SUKHATME. A bit too much—what does that mean ?

PONKSHE. It means—it means that, on the whole, she runs after men too much.

BENARE [*provoking him*]. Tut! tut! tut! Poor man !

SUKHATME. Miss Benare, you are committing contempt of court.

BENARE. The court has gone into that room. So how can contempt of it be committed in this one ? There's not much point in that remark, Sukhatme !

[*Samant laughs heartily.*]

SUKHATME [*to Benare*]. There's no point in coming to grips with you ! Mr Ponkshe . . .

[*Ponkshe has slid out of the witness-box and is talking to Karnik.*]

Nobody at all is serious!

[*Ponkshe returns to the witness-box.*]

Mr Ponkshe, can you tell me—does the accused have a particularly close relationship with any man—married or unmarried ? [*Stressing the words*] Any married or unmarried man ?

BENARE [*interrupting*]. Yes, with the counsel for the prosecution himself ! And with the judge. To say nothing of Ponkshe, Balu here or Karnik.

ROKDE. Miss Benare, I'm warning you, there'll be trouble !

PONKSHE. In these circumstances, Sukhatme, is there any point in continuing this farce of a trial ? Nobody is serious! Kashikar's gone inside. Benare's acting like this. No one lets me speak—

KARNIK. Even the rehearsals for our plays are more serious than this !

3

MRS KASHIKAR. Don't make trouble, Benare. It won't do if tonight's show's a flop because of you.

BENARE. I'm just helping the trial along.

KASHIKAR [*returning*]. What's happened? Sukhatme, continue. Where's my earpick?

BENARE. I think I'll go out for a stroll through the village. You can carry on your trial. Infanticide! Ha! At least I'll get some fresh air.

KARNIK. If that's so, let's call it a day.

MRS KASHIKAR. No. At least let's finish the trial. Let's at least complete the job in hand.

SAMANT [*courteously, to Mrs Kashikar*]. Does that mean it all ends here?

KASHIKAR [*finding his earpick*]. Found it! Come on now. The hearing is to continue. [*Gestures 'Patience!' to Benare*] Sukhatme, what are you waiting for?

SUKHATME. For your earpick to be located, milord. [*Then, striking the alert attitude of a barrister*] Mr Ponkshe—

[*Ponkshe, who has come out of the witness-box, once more enters it hurriedly.*]

Has anything ever struck you about the prisoner's behaviour?

PONKSHE. Yes, a lot.

SUKHATME. What? [*Breathes out smoke.*]

PONKSHE. The prisoner sometimes acts as if she were off her head. That is, there's sometimes no sense at all in her actions.

SUKHATME. For example?

PONKSHE. For example, once she tried to arrange a marriage for me, and—why go further? Right now she's sticking out her tongue like a lunatic! [*Benare hurriedly retracts her tongue.*]

SUKHATME [*as if he has discovered an important clue*]. Good! You can sit down now, Mr Ponkshe—the great scientist. Our next witness is Mr Karnik—the great actor.

[*Ponkshe comes out and, looking steadily at Benare, goes and leans against the wall at one side. Karnik enters the witness-box dramatically, and strikes an attitude.*]

KARNIK. Ask!

SUKHATME. Oath—name—occupation—all over ? Now, Mr
  Karnik, you are an actor ?
KARNIK [*like a witness in a melodrama*]. Yes, and I am
  proud of it.
SUKHATME. Be proud ! But Mr Karnik, do you know this
  lady ? [*Points to Benare.*]
KARNIK [*going through the stage motions of seeing her*]. Yes,
  sir, I—think—I—know—this—lady.
SUKHATME. What do you mean by 'think', Mr Karnik ?
KARNIK. 'Think' means to consider or feel. There's a dic-
  tionary here if you want it.
SUKHATME [*who has moved unconsciously towards the dic-
  tionary, checks himself, and turns.*] I don't need that. Mr
  Karnik, please state definitely whether or not you know
  this lady.
KARNIK [*shrugging his shoulders*]. It's strange ! Sometimes
  we feel we know someone. But in fact we don't. Truth is
  stranger than fiction.
SUKHATME. How did you get to know each other ?
KARNIK. Through this group, you see. We do performances
  of the Living Lawcourt. She's a member. Yes, I remember
  it clearly. [*Theatrical throughout.*]
SUKHATME. What kind of performances are those, Mr
  Karnik ?
KARNIK Smash hits !
SUKHATME [*to Kashikar in a lawyer's tone*]. Milord, I submit that this important statement be noted in the official
  record.
KASHIKAR [*picking his ear*]. It shall be arranged. Proceed.
SUKHATME. Mr Karnik, tell me truthfully. In the plays you
  perform, what is the description of a mother ?
KARNIK. The new plays don't mention them at all. They're
  all about the futility of life. On the whole, that's all man's
  life is.
KASHIKAR. That's it ! That's what I disagree with ! Men
  should have some purpose in life. 'Endless is our zeal for
  striving' should be one's motto. A purpose in life, that's
  what one needs.

SUKHATME. Let that pass. If you had to give a definition of a mother, how would you do it ?

KARNIK [*after he has thought it over*]. A mother is one who gives birth.

SUKHATME. Mr Karnik, who is the mother—the woman who protects the infant she has borne—or the one who cruelly strangles it to death ? Which definition do you prefer ?

KARNIK. Both are mothers. Because both have given birth.

SUKHATME. What would you call motherhood ?

KARNIK. Giving birth to a child.

SUKHATME. But even a bitch gives birth to pups !

KARNIK. Then she's a mother, of course. Who denied it ? Who says only humans can be mothers, and not dogs ?

BENARE [*stretching lazily*]. Bully for you, Karnik !

[*Karnik ignores her.*]

SUKHATME. Karnik's in form today.

KASHIKAR. Show us the form tonight, Karnik. Just now let's have straight answers.

SUKHATME. Mr Karnik, think carefully before you answer my next question. What is your opinion of the prisoner's conduct ?

KARNIK [*after striking two or three tremendous 'thinking' poses*]. Do you mean, in this mock trial, or in real life ?

SUKHATME. In real life, of course.

KASHIKAR [*picking his ear*]. I think it's better if these little questions refer to the trial, Sukhatme.

KARNIK. That's right, is it ? Then it doesn't matter. I don't know anything about the moral conduct of the accused.

SUKHATME. Nothing ? Are you sure ?

KARNIK. Nothing at all. Nothing where the trial is concerned.

[*Benare's expression is tense.*]

SUKHATME. Mr Karnik—[*with sudden fervour*] Have you, in any circumstances, on any occasion, seen the accused in a compromising situation ? Answer yes or no. Yes, or no ?

KARNIK. Not me. But Rokde has.

ROKDE [*confused*]. Me ? I don't know a thing !

SUKHATME [*his chest swelling in great lawyerlike style*]. Mr Karnik, thank you very much. You may take your seat now.

[*Karnik leaves the witness-box.*]

Now, Mr Rokde, please enter the witness-box. Please enter it.

MRS KASHIKAR [*to Samant*]. You're grasping it all, aren't you?

SAMANT. Yes.

ROKDE [*staying where he is, in total confusion*]. Not me!

SUKHATME. Milord, the usher Rokde's evidence is extremely necessary to the trial. He should be summoned to the witness-box without delay.

ROKDE [*wretchedly*]. I won't come! You'll see! I'll go away—

[*Benare is laughing silently.*]

KASHIKAR. Rokde .—

[*Rokde obediently goes and stands in the witness-box. His body is trembling. He is visibly disturbed.*]

PONKSHE [*to Karnik*]. I say, what did he see?

KARNIK. Who says he did? I was just joking, that's all. You passed the buck to me, I passed it to him. The game's got to go on, hasn't it? Sukhatme's, I mean.

SUKHATME. Oath—name—occupation—to continue, Mr Rokde—

[*Rokde is close to tears.*]

Mr Rokde, you heard Mr Karnik refer to you while giving his evidence. Can you throw any further light on that subject?

MRS KASHIKAR. Balu, now give a marvellous, unbroken bit of evidence! If you can manage this, you'll get a chance later on in the show. You'll never get such a big chance again. Watch it all, Samant, watch it carefully.

[*Kashikar glares at her. Mrs Kashikar is silent.*]

SUKHATME. Speak on, Mr Rokde. What did you see?

[*Rokde is genuinely disturbed. He swallows convulsively.*]

Mr Rokde, take God as your witness, and tell me what you saw there.

[*Rokde is speechless.*]

[*Like a lawyer in a film*] Mr Rokde, what did you see in certain important circumstances, on a certain occasion?

Answer me, please.

ROKDE [*with difficulty*]. I saw—hell !

[*This is what he is experiencing at the moment. He is all in a sweat. Benare is laughing unrestrainedly. Karnik winks at Ponkshe.*]

KASHIKAR [*picking his teeth*]. He's been a buffoon like this from the start.

MRS KASHIKAR. Balu, you won't have another chance. Answer him at once ! How dare you be so scared! Shouldn't a man have *some* guts about speaking up in public ? What do you think, Samant ?

SAMANT. But it's difficult...

KASHIKAR. Speak quickly, Balu.

BENARE. Speak, Balu, speak. A—B—C—

ROKDE [*to Benare, furious in spite of his state*]. That's enough ! [*Wipes away sweat repeatedly.*]

SUKHATME [*abandoning his legal voice*]. Mr Rokde—

ROKDE [*stopping him*]. No. Wait a minute. [*He summons up his courage and looks once or twice towards Benare, who is still laughing at him.*] I'll tell you. I went to his house some time ago—

SUKHATME [*in a lawyer's voice*]. Whose house ? Mr Rokde, to whose house did you go ?

ROKDE. Don't keep interrupting me! I went to—to Damle's house !

[*Benare tense.*]

PONKSHE. Our Professor Damle ?

KARNIK. You must have been to his room in the college hostel, you mean ?

ROKDE. Yes. I went there in the evening. As night was falling. And there—*she* was! Miss Benare.

ALL. Who ?

ROKDE [*looking at Benare*]. Now laugh! Make fun of me! This lady was there. Damle and this—Miss Benare !

[*Benare has stiffened. Karnik signals to Ponkshe.*]

SAMANT [*to Mrs Kashikar*]. Is this true, or just for the trial ?

SUKHATME [*with peculiar care*]. Mr Rokde, you went to Professor Damle's house, as night was falling. What did

you see there ? [*in a deep, cruel voice*] What did you see ?
KASHIKAR [*although he is enjoying it all greatly*]. Sukhatme.
I feel this is getting on to too personal a level—
SUKHATME. No, no, no, not at all, milord. It's just for the
trial ; so, Mr Rokde—
BENARE. I don't agree. I'm telling you ! what's all this got
to do with the trial ?
MRS KASHIKAR. But why are you getting into such a state,
Benare ? [*to Kashikar*] Go on.
BENARE. There's no need at all to drag my private life into
this. I can visit whom I like. Damle wasn't eating me up.
SUKHATME. What did you see there, Rokde ? Yes, tell us.
Tell us ! Miss Benare, listen to me. Don't spoil the mood
of the trial. This game's great fun. Just be patient. Now,
Rokde, don't be shy—tell everything you saw.
ROKDE [*looking straight ahead, after a pause*]. They were
sitting there.
SUKHATME. And ?—
ROKDE. What do you mean—and ? They were both sitting
there—in that room.
SUKHATME. What else did you see ?
ROKDE. That's all.
[*Sukhatme is disappointed.*]
But I got such a shock ! Sitting there in Damle's room—the
night falling...
BENARE. What a baby the poor thing is !
ROKDE. Then why did your face fall when you saw me ?
Just explain that ! Damle got rid of me. Without letting me
come in. Usually he always asks me in—into the room !
BENARE [*laughing*] Damle alone knows why he got rid of
you. And do you know why you imagine that my face fell ?
Because Damle snubbed you in front of me. Why should
my face fall ? It stayed right where it should be!
SUKHATME [*to Kashikar*]. Milord, I submit that what the
witness Mr Rokde saw—and he alone knows why he stop-
ed at that—I submit that what he saw be noted in record.
Even to an impartial observer, it reveals that Miss Benare's
behaviour is certainly suspicious.

BENARE. It reveals nothing of the sort! Tomorrow I may
be seen in our Principal's office. Does that mean my behaviour is suspicious? Ha! Our principal is sixty-five!

SUKHATME. Milord, I request that this statement made by
the accused may also be noted, as we wish to introduce
it in evidence.

BENARE. If you like, I'll give you the names and addresses
of twenty-five more people with whom I am alone at times.
Holding a trial, are you? Suspicious, indeed. You don't
even understand the meaning of simple words!

[*Karnik signals to Ponkshe.*]

SUKHATME. Milord, since I consider°that statement, too, to
be valuable, the prosecution requests that it be noted in
evidence.

KASHIKAR [*picking his teeth*]. Which statement? 'You don't
even understand the meaning of words'?

SUKHATME. No—'the names and addresses of 25 people'—
with whom she sometimes—

BENARE. A little while ago, Mr... Mr...Samant and I were
quite alone together. Go on, write his name down, too.
Why don't you?

SAMANT [*rising suddenly, in confusion*]. No, no, this lady
behaved in a most exemplary manner. We just talked of
magic shows—hypnotism and the like—that's all—

SUKHATME. Milord, I request that the reference to hypnotism,
being most important, should be noted in evidence.

KASHIKAR [*picking his teeth*]. But, Sukhatme, to what extent
is all this within the jurisdiction of the court?

KARNIK. This is just a rehearsal, in any case. Just a rehearsal.

PONKSHE. This is just a game. A game, that's all! Which
of us is serious about the trial? It's fun, Sukhatme! Do
go on. [*To Karnik*] I say, this chap seems to be a good
enough lawyer. How's it that his practice is so small?

SAMANT [*to Mrs Kashikar*]. But by hypnotism I only meant—
that is—it was nothing—you know—only ordinary hypnotism—

PONKSHE [*making him sit*]. Do sit down! It's all just a joke.

KARNIK. Sukhatme, don't stop. Let the case go on. Well,

Mrs Kashikar, what do you think, eh?

MRS KASHIKAR. The whole affair's warming up nicely. I wouldn't have imagined... Sukhatme, don't stop; carry on.

SUKHATME [*encouraged by all this*]. Mr Rokde, you may leave the witness-box.

[*Rokde heaves a sigh of relief at this and comes out of the witness-box, to go straight into the inner room*].

Now, Mr Samant.

SAMANT [*standing up, distrustful and confused*]. Me? Did you say me?

SUKHATME. Come.

[*He indicates the witness-box. Samant comes and stands in it.*]

Don't be scared. You just have to answer—

SAMANT.—the questions I'm asked.

SUKHATME. How very clever you are!

MRS KASHIKAR. There are no odds and ends to remember. Besides, this is just a practice trial. The real one is tonight.

SAMANT. Yes, indeed. It's at night. I'm not at all scared. I just get a bit confused, that's all. [*To Sukhatme*] I'll take the oath, just for practice.

SUKHATME. All right. Usher Rokde!

[*Rokde is absent.*]

SAMANT. I think he's gone there, inside. I'll do it myself. [*At a bound, goes and fetches the dictionary. Placing his hand on it*] I, Raghunath Bhikaji Samant, do hereby swear to tell the truth, the whole truth, and nothing but the truth. True enough for the trial, I mean. Of course, what's true for the trial is quite false really. But I'm just taking the oath for practice. [*His hand is still on the dictionary.*] You see, I don't want the sin of falsehood. [*In apologetic tones*] I'm quite religious... The oath's over. Now. [*Enters the witness-box again.*] Go on. [*This is to Sukhatme; then, to Mrs Kashikar*] You see? I'm not frightened. I just get confused because I'm new to all this. [*To Sukhatme*] Well, you may go on.

SUKHATME. Name—occupation—that's all dealt with.

SAMANT. No. Do you want to ask all that? Then go ahead.

SUKHATME. No. Now, Mr—

SAMANT [*proudly*]. Samant. Sometimes people forget my surname. That's why I have to tell it.

SUKHATME. It's all right. Mr Samant, do you know the prisoner, Miss Benare?

SAMANT [*proudly*]. Of course! But not all that well. After all, how well can you get to know a person in two hours or so? But I am acquainted with her. She's a very nice lady.

SUKHATME. But your opinion, or the favourable impression you have formed of her, cannot be regarded as reliable in court, can it?

SAMANT. Yes—No, no, why not? Of course it can. My mother used to be able to sum up a person's worth in just one minute. From his face! Now the poor thing can't see at all. She's grown too old.

[*Rokde enters and takes up his position. Benare is sitting in the dock, her eyes closed, her chin propped up in one hand.*]

She seems to have fallen asleep, Miss Benare. I mean.

BENARE [*her eyes shut*]. I'm awake. I can never, never sleep just when I want to. Never.

SAMANT. I don't have that problem. I can sleep any time I want. [*To Sukhatme*] What about you?

SUKHATME. My sleeping habits are quite different. When I am going to fall asleep it happens in a flash. Otherwise, I lie awake for hours at a stretch.

KASHIKAR [*still picking his teeth and ears*]. Put some corn oil on your head, Sukhatme, and rub it well in. That's what I do. Whatever important social problem there may be, corn oil gives me peaceful sleep. Basically, if your sleep's calm, your brain's bound to be so too. But if your brain's not calm, how on earth will social problems be solved? Most important things, your brain and your digestion. Both of them!

SAMANT. Yes. [*To Sukhatme*] Let's get those questions over with.

SUKHATME. [*picking up the thread with fresh energy*]. Mr—

SAMANT. Samant.

SUKHATME. Mr Rokde saw the accused—Miss Benare—in Professor Damle's room in the evening when it was quite dark.

SAMANT. That's right . . .

SUKHATME. On that occasion, there was no third person there with Professor Damle and the accused.

SAMANT. Correct. But now, do ask me something.

SUKHATME. That's just what I am going to do. Half an hour after that, you reached there.

SAMANT. Where ? No, no! Why, that room's in Bombay ! And I was in this village. Hardly ! It's silly—I don't know your Professor Damle from Adam. How could I get to his room ? Isn't that right ? What are you up to ?

SUKHATME. You reached there.

SAMANT. You've got it all mixed up, counsel . . .

SUKHATME. Mr Samant, for the sake of the trial, we're taking some things for granted.

KARNIK. The crime itself is imaginary. What more do you want ? It's all imaginary . . . that's what it is.

PONKSHE. Only the accused is real !

SAMANT [*to Mrs Kashikar*]. There ! Now I'm in a mess ! [*To Sukhatme*] All right. After half an hour, I reached Professor Damle's room. What next ?

SUKHATME. You tell us that.

SAMANT. How can I tell you ?

SUKHATME. Then who will ?

SAMANT. That's true. I'll have to. But it's hard. The prisoner and Professor Damle. Room . . . evening . . .

PONKSHE. It was quite dark.

KARNIK. Half an hour after that. In other words, when it was very dark. Throughout the college grounds, complete silence . . .

SAMANT [*suddenly*]. Go on, ask me—so I reached there, eh ? I reached there and—and what happened was—the door was locked !

SUKHATME. The door was locked !

SAMANT. Yes. The door was locked. Not from outside. From

inside. And I banged on the door. No, that's wrong. I rang the bell. The door opened. An unknown man stood before me. Guess who it was. Professor Damle! I was seeing him for the first time. So he'd be unknown to me, wouldn't he?

PONKSHE. Bravo, Samant!

MRS KASHIKAR [*to Karnik*]. Oh, he's giving his evidence beautifully!

SAMANT [*gaining confidence*]. Damle was before me. When he saw me, he said with an annoyed expression, 'Yes? Whom do you want?'

PONKSHE [*to Karnik*]. He's describing Damle to the life!

SAMANT. I answered. 'Professor Damle.' He said, 'He's not at home.' And he slammed the door shut. For a second, I stood there stunned. I began to think, should I go home or press the bell once more. Because I had an important errand.

SUKHATME. What?

SAMANT. What?—Well, let's say—something. Let's suppose that I wanted to arrange a lecture by Professor Damle. He does lecture, doesn't he? I only ask, because he is a Professor—so he must lecture at times. So I stood there, wondering how I could go back without arranging the lecture. At that moment I heard a vague sound from the room. Of someone crying.

MRS KASHIKAR. Crying?

SAMANT. Yes. An indistinct sound of crying. It was a woman.

SUKHATME [*excitedly*]. Yes?

SAMANT. For a moment he stood where he was. 'He' means me. He—I mean I—couldn't understand who was crying. You will ask me why I didn't think it was some female member of Professor Damle's family. Well, from the way the woman was crying, she didn't seem to be a member of his family. Why? Because the crying was soft. That is, it was secretive. Now, why would anyone cry secretively in her own house? Thinking over all this, I stood where I was. Just then, I heard some words.

MRS KASHIKAR. Some words?

KARNIK & PONKSHE. Who spoke?

SAMANT. Tut, tut, tut ! You're not supposed to ask. This gentleman—the counsel—will ask me.

SUKHATME. Who spoke ?

SAMANT. The woman, of course. The one inside.

MRS KASHIKAR. Good heavens ! Tell us, do tell us, who was she ? [*Looking unconsciously at Benare.*]

SAMANT. No. He will ask me—the counsel will. Not you.

SUKHATME. I'm asking. Tell us, quick, Mr Samant. What were the words you heard ? Don't waste time. Tell us quick—Mr Samant—be quick !

SAMANT. The words were—shall I tell it all ? ·

SUKHATME. Whatever you can remember—but *tell* us !

SAMANT [*hurriedly looking at a book in his hand*]. 'If you abandon me in this condition, where shall I go ?'

[*Benare is tense.*]

MRS KASHIKAR. Is that really what she said ?

SAMANT. 'How can I tell you ?'

SUKHATME [*snapping at him*]. Then who else on earth can ?

SAMANT. No, no ! I'm telling you the Professor's answer. His answer. Professor Damle's.

SUKHATME. Oh, I see,

SAMANT. 'Where you should go is entirely your problem. I feel great sympathy for you. But I can do nothing. I must protect my reputation.' At that, she said, 'that's all you can talk about, your reputation ? How heartless you are !' He replied, 'Nature is heartless.'

KASHIKAR [*picking his ear fast and furiously*]. I see, I see.

SUKHATME [*staggered*]. Amazing—amazing !—

SAMANTA. 'If you abandon me, I shall have no choice but to take my life.' 'Then do that. I also have no choice. If you kill yourself, I shall be in torment.'

SUKHATME. Simply thrilling !

SAMANT. 'But this threat will not. make me budge an inch from my considered course of action,' he said. She replied, Bear it in mind that you will not escape the guilt of murdering two'—two ?—I'm wrong—no, I'm right ... 'Two living beings.' And then there came a terrifying laugh.

BENARE [*with sudden passion*]. That's enough !

KASHIKAR [*banging his gavel*]. Order, order!

BENARE. It's all a lie! A complete lie!

PONKSHE. Of course it is. So?

KARNIK. Even if it is a lie, it's an effective one!

MRS KASHIKAR. Do go on, Samant.

BENARE. No! Stop all this! Stop it!

SAMANT [*in confusion*]. But what's the matter?

BENARE. This has got to stop! Not a word of it is true!

SAMANT. Of course not.

BENARE. It's all made up! It's a lie!

SAMANT. That's quite right!

BENARE. You're telling barefaced lies!

SAMANTA. What else? [*Brings out the book hidden behind him, and shows it.*] You see, everything I'm saying is out of this!

SUKHATME. Mr Samant, a terrifying laugh...What happened after that?

BENARE. If anyone says one word after this, I—I'll go away!

SUKHATME. Mr Samant...

BENARE. I'll smash up all this! I'll smash it all to bits—into little bits!

MRS KASHIKAR. But my dear Benare, as your conscience is clear, why are you flying into such a violent rage?

BENARE. You've all deliberately ganged up on me! You've plotted against me!

SAMANT. No, no, dear madam, really it's nothing like that!

SUKHATME. Mr Samant, answer. Professor Damle gave a terrifying laugh. Then what did the unknown woman inside the room say?

SAMANT. [*hurriedly consulting his book*]. Wait, I'll find the page and let you know.

BENARE. Samant, if you say one word more—I'll—just you wait.

SUKHATME [*in the right soft and threatening tone*]. Mr Samant . . .

SAMANT. It's quite a problem. I just can't find the page—

SUKHATME [*to Kashikar*]. Milord, the occurrence as it has been related speaks so vividly for itself that there is hardly any need to add anything over and above it. This entire statement should be noted down as part of our evidence against the accused.

KASHIKAR. Request granted.

BENARE Note it down. Note everything down! Just take down note after note! [*Her eyes are suddenly full of tears. Her voice is choked. She is .agitated. Then, with tearful defiance*]. What can you do to me? Just try! [*Tears flow freely from her eyes. Exit into the wings.*]

[*Deeper silence. Except for Samant, everyone's expression changes. A peculiar and cautious excitement breaks out on each face.*]

SAMANT. [*sympathetically*]. Dear, oh dear! Whatever's happened so suddenly to the lady?

KASHIKAR [*picking his ear*]. It's all become quite unexpectedly enjoyable—the whole fabric of society is being soiled these days, Sukhatme. Nothing is undefiled any more.

SUKHATME. That's why thoughtful people like us, Mr Kashikar, should consider these matters seriously and responsibly. This should not be taken lightly.

MRS KASHIKAR. You're absolutely right!

SUKHATME. And if thoughts alone are not enough, we must use deeds. Action! Eh, Karnik?

KARNIK. Yes. Action!

PONKSHE. Right!

SUKHATME. Here, feelings are not enough. We must all get together. We must act.

MRS KASHIKAR. But whatever's happened, really?

KASHIKAR. Keep quiet! What could have happened, Sukhatme? What's your guess?

SUKHATME [*as if he has a fair idea*]. That is the mystery! [*Samant stands there, dismayed.*]

And I think we know the answer to this mystery!

KARNIK
PONKSHE
ROKDE   }—What?
KASHIKAR
MRS KASHIKAR

[*Benare comes out of the inner room and stands in the door-way.*]

SUKHATME [*unconscious of this*]. Well, children, the conclusion's obvious. There's some substance in what Mr Samant said. Even though it came from a book. It holds water!

MRS KASHIKAR. Do you mean that Miss Benare and Professor Da—

SUKHATME. Yes. Beyond a shadow of doubt! There's no question about it.

MRS KASHIKAR. Good gracious!

ROKDE [*now very daring*]. I knew it all along!

SUKHATME. Ssh!

[*Seeing Benare in the doorway, all fall silent. They all look at her. She comes in purposefully and picks up her bag and purse. She goes towards the other door, and unbolts it. All are watching. The door does not open. She pulls at it. It will not open. She starts tugging at it hard. It is locked from outside. She bangs on it with vehemence. And louder. But it is locked. A peculiar joy begins to show on everyone's face but Samant's.*]

SAMANT. There! It's happened! The bolt's slipped shut out-side. That's always the trouble with this door. [*Gets up and goes forward. Struggles with the door.*] If you don't pull the bolt properly to one side when you come in, and then you close the door from inside, you've had it! The door's locked from outside. It's always the case. Try as you will, it just won't open. And what's more, the offices are closed. So there won't be anyone outside just now. [*He bangs on the door again and again.*] It's no use. [*To Miss Benare, who is by him.*] Madam, when you pulled the bolt you did it the wrong way. You should have pulled it back fully. [*He tries giving the door another thump. It's no use. Then coming and standing at one side.*] It's locked!

[*Benare is still standing by the door with her back to the others.*]

KASHIKAR [*cleaning his ears with concentration*]. I think that in the circumstances, Mr Sukhatme, the case should continue.

SUKHATME. [*bowing in legal fashion, with a completely perverse excitement*]. Yes, milord. [*His eyes gleaming.*] Milord, let the accused herself be summoned to the witness-box.

CURTAIN

ACT THREE

[*The same scene. Evening. The cast in the positions they were in at the end of the second act.*]

SUKHATME [*Bowing in the manner of a professional lawyer with a completely perverse excitement*]. Yes, milord, [*His eyes are gleaming.*] Milord, first let the accused herself be summoned to the witness-box.

KASHIKAR. [*Picking his ear*]. Prisoner Miss Benare, enter the witness-box. Enter it, Miss Benare.

[*Benare stands where she is.*]

Incredible ! Such insolence in court ! Usher Rokde, conduct the accused to the witness-box.

ROKDE [*Frightened, trembling a little*]. Me ?

[*Benare stands still.*]

MRS KASHIKAR. Wait, I'll take her. Why do you need him ?

[*She starts pulling Benare along forcibly.*]

Come on, now, Benare.

[*She puts Benare into the witness-box. Benare's face reveals the terror of a trapped animal.*]

SUKHATME [*Looking at Benare as he puts on his gown ceremoniously.*]. Milord, in consideration of the grave aspect which the case before us has assumed, it is my humble submission that if your lordship himself were to wear your gown henceforth, it would appear more decorous.

KASHIKAR. Exactly. Rokde, give me my gown.

[*He puts on the black gown that Rokde unpacks and hands to him. After that, his gravity and dignity increase.*]

SUKHATME. Mr Samant, Mrs Kashikar, Ponkshe, Karnik, seat yourselves there exactly as you should. [*He straightens up, closes his eyes, and meditates for a while. Then, slapping himself piously on the face, he raises his hands to his forehead in prayer twice or thrice.*]

My father taught me the habit, Kashikar, of praying to our family god at the beginning of any new enterprise. How pure it makes one feel ! The mind takes on new strength.

[*He takes one or two steps in the manner of a wrestler who has gained new strength.*] Good ! Now to business. Let the accused take the oath.

[*Rokde comes and stands in front of Benare with the dictionary. Benare is silent. Like a statue.*]

KASHIKAR [*Adjusting his cap*]. Prisoner Miss Benare, take the oath !

[*Benare is silent.*]

SAMANT [*Softly*]. Why not get it over with, Miss Benare ? It's all a game.

[*Benare is silent.*]

MRS KASHIKAR [*Coming forward*]. Give it to me, I'll make her take the oath ; just wait. [*Taking the dictionary from Rokde.*] Benare, say, 'I hereby swear to tell the truth, the whole truth and nothing but the truth.'

[*Benare is silent.*]

KASHIKAR. This is the limit.

MRS KASHIKAR [*Giving the dictionary to Rokde*]: Let's say she's taken the oath. Her hand was on the dictionary. Go on, ask her what you want, Sukhatme.

KASHIKAR. Prisoner Benare, the court hereby warns you. Henceforth there must on no account be any conduct that constitutes contempt of court. Go ahead, Sukhatme !

KARNIK. Fire away !

SUKHATME [*Walking around in front of Benare a while, and suddenly, pointing a finger*]. Your name is Leela Damle.

SAMANT. (*At once*) No—no—Be-na-re. Damle is the Professor.

MRS KASHIKAR. Do listen, Samant. Let her answer.

SUKHATME. Miss Leela Benare—

[*She tries not to listen to or look at him.*]

SUKHATME. Please tell the court your age.

[*He has struck an attitude, confident that she will not tell it. Benare is silent.*]

KASHIKAR. Prisoner Benare, it is your responsibility to answer any questions put to you as a witness. [*Pausing a little*] Prisoner Benare, what are you waiting for ? Answer the question !

MRS KASHIKAR. Why should *she* have to tell her **age** ? I can guess it. Say…it's over thirty-two. A year or so more perhaps, but not less. Just look at her face!

SUKHATME. Thank you, Mrs Kashikar.

KASHIKAR. Wait. What do you mean, 'Thank you, Mrs Kashikar?' The accused has not yet told you her age. I was listening carefully. Prisoner Benare, your age!

MRS KASHIKAR. But I—-

KÁSHIKAR. It is not the custom of any court to accept someone else's answer when the accused is questioned. Don't interrupt! Prisoner at the bar! Answer! Your answer please!

[*Benare is silent.*]

SAMANT. The fact is—it isn't thought—courteous—to ask a lady her age...

KASHIKAR. This is intolerable rudeness! No answer to any question! Is this a court of law, or what is it? [*Bangs the table for effect.*]

PONKSHE. Exactly. This is contempt of court!

KASHIKAR. We will have to take steps to deal with the prisoner's refusal to answer. This is a matter of the court's dignity. The accused will be granted ten seconds to answer. [*Holding his watch in front of him.*] No nonsense, please.

SUKHATME [*In a melodramatic manner, at the end of the tenth second*]. Milord, I withdraw the question. The accused, by her silence, has as good as answered me.

KASHIKAR. All right. She's not less than thirty-four. I'll give it to you in writing! What I say is, our society should revive the old custom of child marriage. Marry off the girls before puberty. All this promiscuity will come to a full stop. If anyone has ruined our society it's Agarkar and Dhondo Keshav Karve. That's my frank opinion, Sukhatme, my frank opinion.

SUKHATME. [*With a lawyerlike bow*]. Yes, milord.

[*Rokde has meanwhile hastily written down Kashikar's sentence in his notebook. Benare is silent in the witness-box.*]

[*Going behind Benare, suddenly*]. Miss Benare.

[*She starts, jerking away from him.*]

Can you tell the court how you came to stay unmarried to such a mature—such an advanced—age? [*Waits; then*] Let me frame my question somewhat differently. How many

chances of marriage have you had so far in your life ? And
how did you miss them ? Tell the court.

KASHIKAR. Answer him ! [*Takes out his watch and holds it
in front of him. She is silent.*] This is really too much !

MRS KASHIKAR. It seems she's decided not to behave herself
and answer properly !

[*Benare is silent.*]

SUKHATME. Milord, I close the examination of the accused
for the time being. It could be resumed at the appropriate
time.

[*Benare leaves the witness-box and goes to the door. It is
locked. Ponkshe blocks the way, so she turns aside. By
then, Mrs Kashikar has caught hold of her, and leads her
to the dock.*]

KASHIKAR. Next witness.

SUKHATME. Mrs Kashikar.

[*At once, Mrs Kashikar eagerly enters the witness-box, tuck-
ing her sari round her fussily as she goes.*]

KASHIKAR. (*To Sukhatme*) Look. That's eagerness for you !
You've hardly called her, and there she is !

MRS. KASHIKAR. You needn't be like *that* ! [*Then, talking
like a stage witness*] I have already taken the oath. Benare
and I—let's say we took it together. And of course I'll
tell the truth. Who's scared ?

SUKHATME. Very well. Mrs Kashikar, can you give me some
information, please ? How did Miss Benare remain unmarried till such a late age ?

MRS KASHIKAR. That's easy ! Because she didn't get married,
of course.

SUKHATME. That's it. But, Mrs Kashikar, at the age of
thirty-two—

KASHIKAR [*Interrupting*]. Thirty-four—count it as thirty-
four !

SUKHATME. How is it that, till the age of thirty-four, an educated, well-brought-up girl—

MRS KASHIKAR. Girl ? You mean 'woman' ! If you call her
a girl—you'd better call me young lady.

SUKHATME. All right. Let's call her a woman then. But, why

isn't she married ? Can you explain that ?

MRS KASHIKAR. Damn the explanation ! Anyone who really wants to can get married in a flash !

SUKHATME. You mean that Miss Benare didn't want to—

MRS KASHIKAR. What else ? That's what happens these days when you get everything without marrying. They just want comfort. They couldn't care less about responsibility ! Let me tell you—in my time, even if a girl was snub-nosed, sallow, hunchbacked, or anything whatever, she—could—still—get—married ! It's the sly new fashion of women earning that makes everything go wrong. That's how promiscuity has spread throughout our society. [*Rokde is jotting it down. To Rokde.*] Finished writing ? [*To Sukhatme.*] Go on. Ask me more.

SUKHATME. You said that this is what happens if you get everything without marrying.

MRS KASHIKAR. Yes, I did.

SUKHATME. What do you mean by 'everything' ? Give me an instance.

MRS KASHIKAR. Well, really ! [*She looks embarrassed.*]

KASHIKAR. [*Picking his ear*]. Come on, don't pretend to be shy, at your age. Just answer his question. You've grown old, but you haven't grown any wiser !

MRS KASHIKAR. My age has nothing to do with it !

KASHIKAR. Answer him !

MRS KASHIKAR. 'Everything' means—everything in this life.

SUKHATME. Don't you feel that to say this about the accused might be unjust ?

MRS KASHIKAR. I Don't think so. We see too many such examples.

SUKHATME. Forget about the others. Have you any proof where Miss Benare is concerned ? Any proof ? Tell me if you have.

MRS KASHIKAR. What better proof ? Just look at the way she behaves. I don't like to say anything since she's one of us. Should there be no limit to how freely a woman can behave with a man ? An unmarried woman ? No matter how well she knows him ? Look how loudly she laughs ! How she sings, dances, cracks jokes ! And wandering alone with how many men, day in and day out !

SUKHATME [*Disappointed at the 'proof'*]. Mrs Kashikar, at the most one can say all this shows how free she is.

MRS KASHIKAR. Free ! Free ! she's free allright—in everything ! I shouldn't say it. But since it's come up in court, I will. Just hold this a minute. [*She puts her knitting into Sukhatme's hands.*] Why must she have Professor Damle, and Damle alone, to see her home after a performance ? Tell me that !

[*Benare is deliberately silent.*]

SUKHATME. [*Brightening up*]. I see—so Miss Benare needs Professor Damle to see her home after a performance ?

[*Ponkshe and Karnik are signalling to each other.*]

MRS KASHIKAR. What else ? Once we—my husband and I— it was just last September—September, wasn't it dear ?

KASHIKAR. No prompting the witness ! You say what you want !

MRS KASHIKAR. Yes, it was September. We both said, 'Come, we'll drop you,' since she was to go home alone. But she very slyly went off with Damle. We looked for her, but she'd vanished !

SUKHATME [*In a lawyer's voice, sounding pleased*]. Peculiar !

MRS KASHIKAR. Just a while back, she was protesting, 'It's a lie ! It's persecution !' Now how's she struck dumb ? That shows you can't suppress the truth. Give me that wool.

SUKHATME. [*Handing over the wool and needles to Mrs Kashikar*]. Mrs Kashikar, Professor Damle is a family man.

MRS KASHIKAR. Yes. He has five children.

SUKHATME. Then how do you know Miss Benare doesn't seek his company innocently, as a responsible elder person ?

MRS KASHIKAR. Then do you mean to say that we—my husband and I—are just vagabonds ? And Damle may be an older man—but what about Balu ?

[*Rokde gives a great start.*]

SUKHATME [*Growing alert*]. What about him, Mrs Kashikar ? What about Rokde ?

[*Benare's expression is tense.*]

MRS KASHIKAR. That's what I'm telling you. After another performance, Benare made overtures to him, too. In the dark. It was he who told me. Didn't you, Balu ?

[*Karnik excepted, commotion all round. Sukhatme is radiant.*]

ROKDE [*Weakly*]. Yes...no...

SAMANT [*To Karnik*]. No, no, she was alone with me a little while ago, and,...

[*Karnik silences him.*]

SUKHATME. Mrs Kashikar, you may step down. Your evidence is complete. Milord, I submit that Rokde be called once more to give evidence.

[*Rokde cringes where he is. Sukhatme strolls over to stand near Benare. In confidential tones.*] Miss Benare, the game's really warmed up, hasn't it ?

KASHIKAR. Rokde, come and give evidence.

[*Rokde hesitantly goes to the witness-box without looking at Benare.*]

MRS KASHIKAR. [*As he passes*]. Balu, speak the truth ! Don't be afraid.

SUKHATME [*Going towards the witness-box*]. Mr Rokde— you've already taken the oath. Well, Mr Rokde, in the course of her evidence, Mrs Kashikar has made a most disturbing statement about you and the accused.

[*Rokde begins to shake his head.*]

MRS KASHIKAR. Balu ! Didn't you tell me so ?

SUKHATME. Mr Rokde, whatever happened after the performance that night, good or bad, pleasant or unpleasant, tell it all to the court. That is your duty. The performance ended. What happened then ?

ROKDE. [*Feebly*]. I—I—

SUKHATME. After the performance all of us left the hall. Then— ?

KARNIK. And only these two remained behind.

MRS KASHIKAR. Then it seems, she took his hand—Balu's, I mean.

PONKSHE. Gosh !

SUKHATME. And then ? What did she do then, Rokde ?

What more did she do ? What next ?

MRS KASHIKAR. I'll tell you !

KASHIKAR. No, you won't. Let him tell it. Don't interrupt all the time !

SUKHATME. Yes, Mr Rokde—tell it bravely—don't be afraid.

KASHIKAR. Afraid ? Why should he be ? There's some law and order here, isn't there ?

[*Rokde takes stock of the situation. Then, realizing he has enough protection against Benare, he plucks up courage.*]

ROKDE. [*Bravely*]. She held my—my hand.

SUKHATME. Yes ?

ROKDE. So, then—So then I said—'This isn't proper. It's not proper ! —I —I don't like this at all— it doesn't become you'—That's—that's what I said !

SUKHATME. And then ?

ROKDE. I freed my hand. She moved away. She said, Don't tell anyone what happened.

BENARE. That's a lie !

KASHIKAR [*Banging the gavel*]. Order! The accused is sternly reprimanded for disturbing the proceedings of the court. Continue, Rokde, continue.

ROKDE. If you tell anyone, I'll do something to you. That's what she said to me, Anna.

SUKHATME. When did this happen, Mr Rokde ?

ROKDE. Eight days ago, when we had our show at Dombivli.

SUKHATME. Milord, this means that the accused committed an outrage in a lonely spot, on a boy like Rokde, much younger than her—almost like her younger brother. Not only that, but she threatened him with consequences if the matter came to light. She tried to cover up her sinful deed !

MRS KASHIKAR. But the truth will out.

SUKHATME. So, Rokde, the accused threatened to harm you somehow. What next ? What happened then ?

ROKDE [*Unconsciously raising one hand to his cheek*]. I— I slapped her !

PONKSHE. What ?

KARNIK. How melodramatic !

ROKDE. Yes—I said, 'What do you take me for ? Do what-

ever you like! I won't stay quiet about this.' That's why
I told Mrs Kashikar. Yes, that's why.

KASHIKAR. Go on, tell her everything, Rokde; don't tell anything to *me*!

ROKDE [*Indistinctly*]. I'm sorry, Anna. I was wrong. I thought
—I thought, in any case you'd find out—from Mrs Kashikar
here, I mean—so I—

SUKHATME. What happened next, Rokde? What next?

ROKDE. Then?—then nothing. That's all. Can I go?

SUKHATME. Yes, Mr Rokde.

[*Takes a scrap of paper out of his pocket, and writes on
it, muttering loudly, 'Eight days ago, the performance at
Dombivli.' Rokde hastily leaves the witness-box, and stands
at a distance, wiping the sweat from his face. His expression
is calm and satisfied.*]

MRS KASHIKAR. But you hadn't told me this last bit, Balu—
about slapping her!

SAMANT [*To Ponkshe*]. Impossible! I can't believe it!

[*A pronounced excitement is in the air.*]

PONKSHE [*From his seat, puffing hard at his pipe*]. Sukhatme, my evidence now—call me as a witness! Call me
now!

[*His gaze is on the hapless Benare. ...His tone is impatient.*]
Just call me!

KASHIKAR. Sukhatme, call Ponkshe. Let's hear him...call
him now. Let's hear him once and for all!

SUKHATME. Mr Ponkshe be called to the witness-box!

ROKDE. Next witness, Mr Ponkshe!

[*Ponkshe enters the witness-box.*]

PONKSHE. Shall I take the oath again? I hereby place my
hand upon the Oxford English Dictionary, and swear that
I—

KASHIKAR. It's understood. Sukhatme, proceed.

SUKHATME. Mr Ponkshe, the accused, Miss Benare—

PONKSHE [*Gazing at Benare*].—is what I have something
important to tell you about.

[*Benare stiffens where she is.*]
Just ask her this. Why does she keep a bottle of TIK-20 in

her purse ?

[*Benare flinches.*]

MRS KASHIKAR. What more now !

PONKSHE. That is a powerful bedbug poison. It's famous.

SAMANT [*To Karnik*]. Perhaps she was taking it home—

SUKHATME. Can you tell us, Mr Ponkshe, how and when you first found out that the accused was carrying such a terrible poison as TIK-20 in her purse ?

[*Benare has tensed completely.*]

PONKSHE. Yes. One of her little pupils stays in my tenement. About ten days ago, she came to me and said, our teacher's sent you this.

KASHIKAR. TIK-20 ?

PONKSHE. No, a note in a sealed envelope. I opened it. Inside there was another envelope. That, too, was sealed. There was a slip of paper in it, which said, 'Will you meet me, please ? I have something to discuss with you. Come at a quarter past one. Wait in the Udipi restaurant just beyond the school.' Of course, I didn't like it at all. But I said to myself, let's see what her game is. So I went along. Just for the heck of it.

Five minutes later, Miss Benare came there hurriedly, looking quite guilty.

[*Benare has tensed still more.*]

SUKHATME. I see—

KASHIKAR. Then ? What happened then, Ponkshe ?

PONKSHE. She said, 'Not here—in public—someone'll see us—let's go into a family room.'

MRS KASHIKAR [*Sarcastically*]. Magnificent!

PONKSHE. So we sat in a 'family room.' We ordered tea. When Miss Benare's problem had been discussed, she opened her purse to take out her handkerchief. And out of it there rolled a small bottle—

[*For a moment, there is silence.*]

SUKHATME. A bottle of TIK-20 ! Good! But Mr Ponkshe, what had happened between you and Miss Benare before that ? I mean, what was the thing she wanted to discuss with you ? You haven't told us that.

[*Benare is shaking her head with silent vehemence, telling him not to do so.*]

PONKSHE. She made known her desire to marry me.

KARNIK.   What ?

KASHIKAR.   What ?

[*Rokde and the others are astounded.*]

KASHIKAR. This appears terribly interesting, Sukhatme.

SUKHATME. True, milord, it is and it will be. [*His famished lawyer's gaze is on Benare.*] Did she tell you she was in love with you, etc. ?

PONKSHE. No. But she told me she was pregnant.

[*Sensation. Benare is sitting like a block of stone, drained of colour and totally desolate.*]

KARNIK. Are you telling the truth, Ponkshe ?

PONKSHE. What do you think ? That I'm lying ?

KASHIKAR. Who was the father—continue, Ponkshe, continue —don't stop there !

SUKHATME. Mr Ponkshe—

PONKSHE. Miss Benare made me promise never to tell anyone the name of the man who—so she said—had made her pregnant. So far I've kept my word.

MRS KASHIKAR. But who *was* it ?

KASHIKAR. What'll you take to shut up ? The cat'll be out of the bag soon, anyway. Don't be so impatient ! But what I don't understand, Ponkshe, is why, if Miss Benare was pregnant by one man, she expressed a desire to marry another—I mean, to marry you !

PONKSHE. Exactly.

SUKHATME. What was your answer, Mr. Ponkshe ? Were you prepared to take a broad view of things for the sake of humanity, and accept the child along with the mother ?

PONKSHE. The answer is quite clear.

SUKHATME. You weren't prepared, of course.

PONKSHE. No, I wasn't.

SUKHATME. And it was after this, Mr Ponkshe, that the bottle of TIK-20 rolled out of Miss Benare's purse !

PONKSHE. Of course ! I myself picked it up and returned it to her. Shall I give you the whole conversation ? If you want I'll tell that too.

BENARE. [*Shooting up on to her feet*]. No! No!

KASHIKAR [*Banging his gavel*]. Silence! Mr Ponkshe, give us the conversation. [*To Sukhatme.*] Now we'll hear the name—

BENARE. No! You promised, Ponkshe!

SUKHATME. Mr Ponkshe, what indeed could the conversation have been, for Miss Benare to be so agonized?

KASHIKAR. Tell us, Ponkshe—don't wait—tell it quick—this is a matter of social importance.

PONKSHE. But she won't like it.

KASHIKAR [*Banging the gavel*]. Who is the judge here, Ponkshe? Since when has the question of the accused's likes and dislikes being admitted in court? When? I say to you—continue!

BENARE. [*Coming in front of Ponkshe*]. Ponkshe—

KASHIKAR [*Banging the gavel*]. Order! The accused to the dock! To the dock! Rokde, conduct the accused to the dock!

[*Rokde moves forward a little and halts.*]

BENARE. Just you tell it and you'll see, Ponkshe—

KASHIKAR. Prisoner at the bar, go to the dock—Rokde, take her to the dock...

MRS KASHIKAR [*Coming forward and grasping Benare's hand*]. First stand over there. Come on, Rokde, hold her hand.

[*Rokde lingers behind them.*]

Come, Benare ; come on.

[*She drags her to the dock. Mrs Kashikar and Rokde stand guard.*]

Discipline means discipline.

KASHIKAR. Speak, Mr. Ponkshe, What was your conversation about? Where's my earpick? [*He finds it.*] Go on. Mr Ponkshe, what was it about?

PONKSHE. First, we chatted aimlessly. 'Sukhatme's a good man, but he's smothered by ill luck, poor chap. His practice is poor ; —he just sits in the barristers' room playing patience—they say it's well known that if you take your

case to him, it's jail for certain! —he just goes dumb
before the judge...'

SUKHATME [*Swallowing his rage and sense of insult*]. I see
...yes, go on—

PONKSHE. '...Kashikar torments poor Rokde. Because he
constantly suspects an entanglement between him and his
wife. Because they have no children, you see ...'

MRS KASHIKAR. Is that what she said ?

[*Highly offended, she looks daggers at Benare.*]

MR KASHIKAR [*Picking his ear vigorously*]. Go on, tell us
more, Ponkshe—

PONKSHE. After some talk of this nature, we came to the
real issue.

KARNIK. Wait. What did she say about me, Ponkshe ?

PONKSHE. Nothing.

KARNIK. She must have said something—that I'm a rotten
actor, or something. I know what she thinks of me. I know
it well.

PONKSHE. She asked jokingly ; 'Well, are you fixed up somewhere ?' So I said, 'Unless I find someone just to my
taste, I'm not interested in marrying.' So she asked, 'What
exactly do you mean by "to your taste" ? What do you
look for ?' I replied, 'On the whole, girls are silly and
frivolous—that's my opinion. I want a mature partner.'
Then she asked, 'Don't you think that maturity—that is, a
fully developed understanding—comes to a person only
with experience ?' 'I don't know,' I replied. She then said,
'And experience comes with age, with a slightly unusual
way of life. And this sort of experience is never happy or
pleasing. It gives pain to the person who gains it. And it's
usually intolerable to others. But will you bear with it ?
I mean, supposing it is a really mature person. Older than
you and more educated ?' 'I haven't yet thought seriously
about it.' 'Then you should,' she replied. So I asked
whether she had some promising bride in mind. She said,
'Yes. I feel she's the kind you want. You just have to
understand her unusualness.' I couldn't see why she was
making this great effort to get me married. I asked casually,

'What sort of unusualness do you mean?' She replied,
'The girl's just gone through a shattering heartbreak, and'
—wait, I'll think of the exact words—yes—'the fruit of
that love'—here she stumbled a little—'is in her womb.
Actually it is no fault of hers. But her situation's very
serious indeed. She wants to bring up the child. In fact it's
only for the· child she wants to go on living and get
married.' She spoke some more in the same vein. I grew
suspicious. So in order to get the truth out of her, I said,
'Oh! poor girl! Her luck seems really bad. Who is the
scoundrel responsible?'

SUKHATME. Thereupon she said it was Professor Damle!

PONKSHE. No. First she said, 'Please don't call him a scoundrel. He may be a good man. He may be very great and
wise. She may have fallen short. She may not have been
able to convince him how deeply she feels for him. The
woman is not the crucial factor. It's the baby that comes
first.'

SUKHATME. And then?

PONKSHE. Then she said, 'She worshipped that man's
intellect. But all he understood was her body.' She added
other things. On the same lines. How she couldn't find a
place in Damle's life. His—

SAMANT. }
KARNIK. } Damle's?
SUKHATME. }

KASHIKAR [*Banging on the table*]. The cat's out of the bag!

PONKSHE. To tell you the truth, I was bound by oath not to
tell the name, but—

SUKHATME. Doesn't matter, Mr Ponkshe, it doesn't matter
at all. It's no sin to break your oath inadvertently—at least,
not in court. So the child she's carrying is Professor
Damle's? Go on, go on—

PONKSHE. Then she fell at my feet.

KASHIKAR. I see—I see—

PONKSHE. Yes, she fell at my feet. And I said, 'This doesn't
become you, Miss Benare. It's an insult to have asked me

this at ail. Do you think I'm so worthless ?' When she saw
my face, she got up at once, and said, laughing, 'Did you
really think I was telling the truth ? It was just a joke !
That's all !' Then she burst out laughing.

MRS KASHIKAR. A joke, did she say !

PONKSHE. But she had tears in her eyes. That made everything
quite clear. Then she went off in a hurry saying she was
late.

SUKHATME. Thank you, Mr Ponkshe, for your valuable
evidence.

[Ponkshe comes out of the witness-box. Sukhatme takes out
the piece of paper, and muttering loudly, notes down, 'Ten
days before the incident of holding Rokde's hand.']

That's fine. Milord, this evidence needs no comment. It's
so clear—and. I may add, so self-evident. The accused
first accosted Mr Ponkshe. When she realized there was
nothing doing in that quarter, she committed the outrage
on Rokde. The next witness will be the accused, milord.

[He points to Benare. She looks half-dead.]

KARNIK [Raising his hand in a stagey gesture]. Wait! Wait!
I have something important to disclose regarding the case.

SUKHATME. Mr Karnik, into the box.

[He walks theatrically into it. Mr Kashikar is picking his
ear vigorously.]

SUKHATME. Speak, Mr Karnik. What do you wish to tell
the court ?

KARNIK [Stagily]. The evidence given to the court by Rokde
concerning the accused, Miss Benare, and himself, is
incorrect.

ROKDE [In a whining tone]. What business is it of yours ?

KARNIK. [Stagily]. Because, by chance, I happened to be a
witness of what was said and done on that occasion.

KASHIKAR. [Cleaning his earpick]. Which one ? Tell us what
you have to, without complicating the issue...

KARNIK. [Dramatically]. Life itself is a complication these
days. The Western playwright Ionesco—

KASHIKAR [Banging his gavel]. To the point ! Don't digress !
Stick to the point !

KARNIK. I only mentioned him because the subject of complications cropped up—

SUKHATME. What amendment would you suggest, Mr. Karnik, to what has been stated before the court, regarding the accused and Rokde ?

KARNIK. As God is my witness, I must state that Rokde did not slap the accused.

ROKDE [*Whining*]. It's a lie !

KARNIK. What happened was roughly like this. The accused accosted Rokde. I saw that. So I stood aside in the darkness to see how it would develop. The accused asked, 'Then what have you decided ?' Rokde's answer came over, 'I can't do anything without Mrs Kashikar's permission. Don't press me.' The accused then said, 'How much more of your life will you spend under Mrs Kashikar's thumb ?' Rokde replied, 'I can't help it. That's one's luck. I can't think of marriage.' The accused said to him, 'Think again. I'll support you. You won't lack for anything then. You won't have to fear Mr and Mrs Kashikar. You'll be independent.' Rokde replied, 'I'm scared. And if I marry you when you're in this condition, the whole world'll sling mud at me. No one in my family's done a thing like that. Don't depend on me. Or else I'll have to tell Mrs Kashikar.' Upon this, the accused, in a rage—

ROKDE. It's a lie !

KARNIK. —struck Rokde in the face.

[*Rokde's hand has unconsciously gone to his cheek.*]

ROKDE. It's a lie—a barefaced lie !

[*Mrs Kashikar is glaring at him.*]

SUKHATME. Thank you, Mr Karnik. This means that it is true the accused was pressing Rokde to marry her. The only difference in what you say is about who slapped whom.

KARNIK. Not just what I say—but what I saw.

SUKHATME. That's so, Mr Karnik [*Showing him the way out of the witness-box*]—

KARNIK. I have something more to say.

KASHIKAR. If it isn't anything useless and irrelevant, let's
5

hear it. No complications.

KARNIK. Milord—

KASHIKAR [*Banging the gavel*]. Order! what do you think
you are? A lawyer? Just say 'Your lordship' like any
other witness!

KARNIK. Your lordship—

KASHIKAR. That's it. That's the way. Speak. But no complications! We want everything straight and simple.

ROKDE. [*Piteously, to Mrs Kashikar, in a soft voice*].
Mrs Kashikar—

MRS KASHIKAR. Don't speak to me at all!

ROKDE. But Mrs Kashikar!...

[*She turns her head away. Rokde is still more miserable.*]

KARNIK. Your lordship, I happen to know a cousin of the
accused's. I mean, I just got to know him by chance,
at a cricket match at the Dadar Gymkhana. A common
friend of ours was playing in the Bachelors' Eleven. My
friend's friend turned out to be the cousin of the accused
—so my friend told me. My friend knows the accused. I
mean, not personally, but a lot of people know the accused,
and like them, so did he. I mean, he knew *about* the accused.

KASHIKAR. I see. And with whom are you chatting like this?
Show respect to the court.

KARNIK [*Striking the attitude of respecting the court*]. Yes.
Well then, the cousin of the accused and I—we had just
met—the subject casually came up. He gave me some important information.

SUKHATME. For instance?

KARNIK. For instance, the accused had attempted suicide
once before.

SUKHATME [*Radiant*]. That's the point! There is a precedent for the bottle of TIK-20.

KARNIK. I can't say that exactly. I can only tell you what
happened. My information is that the accused attempted
suicide because of a disappointment in love. She fell in
love at the age of fifteen, with her own maternal uncle!
That's what ended in disappointment.

MRS KASHIKAR [*Totally floored*]. Her uncle !

SUKHATME. Milord—her maternal uncle—her mother's brother. What an immoral relationship !

KASHIKAR. In other words, just one step away from total depravity. Fine, Sukhatme, very fine!

SUKHATME. Milord, why do you say 'fine' ? The present conduct of the accused is totally licentious. We know that. But it now seems that her past, too, is smeared in sin. This shows it as clear as daylight.

[*Benare struggles to her feet and tries to reach the door. Mrs Kashikar grasps her and forces her back to the dock.*]

MRS KASHIKAR. Where d'you think you're going ? The door's locked ! Sit down !

KARNIK. I've finished.

[*Bowing dramatically to Kashikar, he leaves the witness-box and returns to his place.*]

KASHIKAR [*Banging his hand suddenly on the table as if he has all of a sudden remembered something.*] There's no doubt at all, Sukhatme ! No doubt.

SUKHATME. About what, milord ?

KASHIKAR. I'll tell you ! Sukhatme, I wish to set aside the tradition of the court, and give an important piece of evidence.

SUKHATME. Milord ?

KASHIKAR. This case has great social significance, Sukhatme. No joking ! I must put aside the practice of court, and give evidence. Sukhatme, ask my permission. Ask me. Ask!

SUKHATME. Milord, considering the importance of the case, I humbly submit that tradition should be broken, to allow the judge's worshipful self to enter the witness-box.

KASHIKAR. Permission granted. [*He comes and stands in the witness-box.*] Examine me. Come on. [*He is bursting to speak. His eyes are on Benare.*] Not a doubt of it !

SUKHATME [*Striking a lawyer's attitude*]. Mr Kashikar, your occupation ?

KASHIKAR. Social worker.

SUKHATME. Do you know the accused ?

KASHIKAR. Only too well ! A sinful canker on the body of

society—that's my honest opinion of these grown-up un-married girls.

SUKHATME [*Taking an even more typical lawyer's pose*]. Do not give your opinion unless you are asked, Mr Kashikar!

KASHIKAR. An opinion's an opinion. I don't wait for any-one's permission to give it.

PONKSHE. Bravo !

SUKHATME. Don't wait for it, then. Mr Kashikar, can you place before the court any important evidence about the charge that has been made here against the accused ?

KASHIKAR. Well, that's why I'm standing here !

SUKHATME. Then speak.

KASHIKAR [*Looking at Benare*]. I often have cause to visit the famous leader Nanasaheb Shinde of Bombay. Of course, the bond between us is that of a common love for social work. Besides, he is the Chairman of the Education Society. Well, his greatness is different from mine. That's not the question here. But recently at his house, say at about nine o'clock at night—when I was sitting there to discuss some work, I heard conversation in the next room. [*Benare starts.*] One of the voices was Nanasaheb's. But the other voice, too, seemed familiar.

MRS KASHIKAR. Whose was it ?

KASHIKAR. Sukhatme, give her a reprimand, go on. You mustn't interrupt a witness ! Before I could tell whose the other voice was, the conversation was over. In a little while Nanasaheb came out. In the course of our conversa-tion I asked about it. He replied, 'A school-mistress from our Education Society's High School had come here. She comes here continually. She wants us to drop an enquiry against her. She's a young woman. So I couldn't say no straight away. I have called her again, for a quiet talk.' Of course, I was still curious who this woman could be. Though Nanasaheb did not tell me, I have just realized that the woman, far from being some stranger, was this one—I mean, she was Miss Benare ! I am 101 per cent certain ! The same voice exactly. Not a doubt of it !

MRS KASHIKAR. Good gracious !

MR KASHIKAR Ask me, Sukhatme, how I'm so certain. This very morning I took over a garland of flowers to Nanasaheb's house, as it's his birthday. There Nanasaheb was talking angrily to someone on the phone, 'It is a sin to be pregnant before marriage. It would be still more immoral to let such a woman teach, in such a condition ! There is no alternative—this woman must be dismissed,' he was saying. Finally, he instructed, 'Send the order for my signature this very day !'

[*A shock for Benare.*]

Now who else comes to your mind ? Tell me ! I *say* it was Miss Benare !

SAMANT. Dear, oh dear! Is she going to lose her job ?

SUKHATME. It can't be helped. Tit for tat ! As you sow, so shall you reap ... that's the rule of life. [*Rokde opens his notebook and writes it down.*] But Mr Kashikar, what made you think *that* woman was this one—was positively our Miss Benare ?

KASHIKAR. My dear man, do you take me for a child, that I shouldn't understand such a simple thing ? I've been studying society for the last forty years. I'll have you know ! A word to the wise is enough ! There is not the slightest doubt in my mind that I've guessed right. It was definitely Miss Benare. Just see whether or not she gets that order tomorrow, that's all ! Order for dismissal ! that's all I wanted to record here. [*He leaves the witness-box and seats himself on the judge's chair.*] The prosecution may continue.

[*A small bottle is in Benare's hand. Just as she is about to put it to her mouth, Karnik dashes forward and strikes it away. The bottle rolls towards Ponkshe's feet.*]

PONKSHE. [*Picking it up and looking at it, then putting it on the judge's table*]. TIK-20.

[*Samant is shocked. Kashikar looks at the bottle and takes charge of it.*]

KASHIKAR. The prosecution may continue.

SUKHATME. With this last and most important piece of evidence, the testimony for the prosecution is complete.

Milord, the case for the prosecution rests. [*He goes and sits down in his chair, as if exhausted.*]

KASHIKAR [*With all the gravity of a judge*]. Counsel for the accused !

[*Sukhatme goes and sits with lowered head on the stool reserved for the counsel for the accused.*]

Call the witnesses for your side!

SUKHATME [*Getting up with the gesture of a tired man, makes a lawyer-like bow and in equally exhausted tones. says*]. Yes, milord. Our first witness is Professor Damle.

ROKDE. [*Acting the usher*]. Damle ! Professor Damle ! [*To Kashikar*] Professor Damle is absent.

KASHIKAR. [*To Sukhatme*]. Next witness, please.

SUKHATME. Our next witness is Nanasaheb Shinde.

KASHIKAR. [*Picking his teeth*]. Absent ! How could *he* come here ? Next—

SUKHATME. The other member of this group, Mr Rawte—

KASHIKAR. He is absent, too. Are those all the witnesses for the defence ?

SUKHATME. I wish to cross-examine the witness for the prosecution, milord.

KASHIKAR. Permission refused. Take your seat.

SUKHATME. [*Sighing*]. The case for the accused rests. [*Goes and seats himself on the stool kept for the counsel for the accused.*]

KASHIKAR [*Spitting out something*]. Good! Now counsel for the prosecution, plead your case. Don't waste time, now.

[*Sukhatme changes his place. Sits down energetically on his previous chair. Then springs to his feet like a wrestler and comes forward.*]

KASHIKAR. Be brief.

SUKHATME [*Now the counsel for the prosecution*]. Milord, the nature of the charge against the accused, Miss Leela Benare, is truly dreadful. The woman who is an accused has made a heinous blot on the sacred brow of motherhood—which is purer than heaven itself. For that, any punishment, however great, that the law may give her, will be too mild by far. The character of the accused is appalling. It is bankrupt

of morality. Not only that. Her conduct has blackened all
social and moral values. The accused is public enemy num-
ber one. If such socially destructive tendencies are encouraged to flourish, this country and its culture will be totally
destroyed. Therefore, I say the court must take a very stern,
inexorable view of the prisoner's crime, without being trapped in any sentiment. The charge against the accused is one
of infanticide. But the accused has committed a far more
serious crime. I mean unmarried motherhood. Motherhood
without marriage has always been considered a very great
sin by our religion and our traditions. Moreover, if the
accused's intention of bringing up the offspring of this un-
lawful maternity is carried to completion, I have a dreadful
fear that the very existence of society will be in danger.
There will be no such thing as moral values left. Milord,
infanticide is a dreadful act. But bringing up the child of
an illegal union is certainly more horrifying. If it is encouraged, there will be no such thing as the institution of
marriage left. Immorality will flourish. Before our eyes, our
beautiful dream of a society governed by tradition will crum-
ble into dust. The accused has plotted to dynamite the very
roots of our tradition, our pride in ourselves, our culture
and our religion. It is the sacred and imperative duty of
your Lordship and every wise and thoughtful citizen amongst
us to destroy that plot at once. No allowance must be made
because the accused is a woman. Woman bears the grave
responsibility of building up the high values of society. *'Na
stri swatantryamarhati.'* 'Woman is not fit for independence.'
...That is the rule laid down for us by tradition. Abiding
by this rule, I make a powerful plea. *'Na Miss Benare
swatantryamarhati.'* 'Miss Benare is not fit for independence.' With the urgent plea that the court should show
no mercy to the accused, but give her the greatest and
severest punishment for her terrible crime, I close the
argument for the prosecution.

KASHIKAR. Good ! Counsel for the accused ! The accused's
lawyer !

⌜*Sukhatme assumes that character and changes his place.*

rising once more with a downcast face.]

SUKHATME [*Walking forward with heavy steps, and in a tone full of false emotion*]. Milord, that the crime is very serious, I do not dispute. But consider this. Man is, in the last analysis, prone to error. Youth leads a person astray. Let the terrible crime that the accused has committed and is committing, be regarded with mercy. Mercy, milord— for humanity's sake, mercy.

[*He has come to the judge's table. Benare is motionless.*]

KASHIKAR. Good. Now, prisoner Benare—

[*She is quite still.*]

Prisoner Benare, before the sentence is pronounced, have you anything to say about the charge that has been made against you? [*Putting forward his watch*] The accused will be given ten seconds.

[*She is as motionless as before. From somewhere in the background, music can be heard. The light changes. The whole court 'freezes' in the positions they are in at the moment. And the motionless Benare stands up erect.*]

BENARE. Yes, I have a lot to say. [*Stretches to loosen her arms.*] For so many years, I haven't said a word. Chances came, and chances went. Storms raged one after another about my throat. And there was a wail like death in my heart. But each time I shut my lips tight. I thought, no one will understand. No one *can* understand! When great waves of words came and beat against my lips, how stupid everyone around me, how childish, how silly they all seemed. Even the man I call my own. I thought, I should just laugh and laugh till I burst. At all of the them…that's all—just laugh and laugh! And I used to cry my guts out. I used to wish my heart would break! My life was a burden to me. [*Heaving a great sigh*] But when you can't lose it, you realize the value of it. You realize the value of living. You see what happiness means. How new, how wonderful every moment is! Even *you* seem new to yourself. The sky, birds, clouds, the branch of a dried-up tree that gently bends in, the curtain moving at the window, the silence all around—all sorts of distant, little noises,

even the strong smell of medicines in a hospital, even that
seems full to bursting with life. Life seems to sing for you !
There's great joy in a suicide that's failed. It's greater even
than the pain of living. [*Heaves a deep sigh.*] Throw your
life away—and you realize the luck of having it. Guard it
dearer than life—and it only seems fit to throw away.
Funny, isn't it ? Look after it. And you feel like throwing
it away. Throw it away—and you're blissfully happy it's
saved ! Nothing satisfies. The same thing, again and again.
[*In a classroom manner.*] Life is like this. Life is so and
so. Life is such and such. Life is a book that goes ripping
into pieces. Life is a poisonous snake that bites itself. Life
is a betrayal. Life is a fraud. Life is a drug. Life is drud-
gery. Life is a something that's nothing—or a nothing
that's something. [*Suddenly striking a courtroom attitude.*]
Milord, life is a very dreadful thing. Life must be hanged.
Na jeevan jeevanamarhati. 'Life is not worthy of life'. Hold
an enquiry against life. Sack it from its job ! But why ?
Why ? Was I slack in my work ? I just put my whole
life into working with the children...I loved it ! I taught
them well ! I knew that life is no straightforward thing.
People can be so cruel. Even your own flesh and blood
don't want to understand you. Only one thing in life is
all-important—the body ! You may deny it, but it is true.
Emotion is something people talk about with sentiment.
It was obvious to me. I was living through it. It was burn-
ing through me. But—do you know ? —I did not teach
any of this to those tender, young souls. I swallowed that
poison, but didn't even let a drop of it touch them ! I
taught them beauty. I taught them purity. I cried inside,
and I made them laugh. I was cracking up with despair,
and I taught them hope. For what sin are they robbing me
of my job, my only comfort ? My private life is my own
business. I'll decide what to do with myself ; everyone
should be able to ! That can't be anyone else's business ;
understand ? Everyone has a bent, a manner, an aim in
life. What's anyone else to do with these ? [*At once, in
the light, playful mood she has at school.*] Hush ! Quiet

there ! Silence ! What a noise ! [*Comes out of the witness-box and wanders as if in class.*] Sit still as statue ! [*She is looking at each figure frozen still.*] Poor things ! Children, who are all these ? [*Light illuminates each face one by one. They all look fearsome, silent, ghostlike.*] These are the mortal remains of some cultured men of the twentieth century. See their faces—how ferocious they look ! Their lips are full of lovely worn-out phrases ! And their bellies are full of unsatisfied desires.

[*Sound of the hourly bell at school. A distant noise of children chattering. For a moment, she is silent and concentrates on the sound. She loses herself in it. The sound then recedes and is heard no more. Silence. Looking around her as if she is walking up, she is suddenly terrified of the silence.*] No, no ! Don't leave me alone ! I'm scared of them. [*Terrified, she hides her face and trembles.*] It's true, I did commit a sin. I was in love with my mother's brother. But in our strict house, in the prime of my un-folding youth, he was the one who came close to me. He praised my bloom every day. He gave me love. . . . How was I to know that if you felt like breaking yourself into bits and melting into one with someone—if you felt that just being with him gave a whole meaning to life—and if he was your uncle, it was a sin ! Why, I was hardly fourteen ! I didn't even know what sin was—I swear by my mother, I didn't ! [*She sobs loudly like a little girl.*] I insisted on marriage. So I could live my beautiful lovely dream openly. Like everyone else ! But all of them—my mother too—were against it. And my brave man turned tail and ran. Such a rage—I felt such a rage against him them—I felt like sma-shing his face in public and spitting on it ! But I was ignorant. Instead, I threw myself off a parapet of our house—to embrace death. But I didn't die. My body didn't die ! I felt as if feelings were dead—but they 'hadn't died either then. Again, I fell in love. As a grown woman. I threw all my heart into it ; I thought, this will be different. This love is intelligent. It is love for an unusual intellect. It isn't love at all—it's worship ! But it was the same mistake.

I offered up my body on the altar of my worship. And my intellectual god took the offering—and went his way. He didn't want my mind, or my devotion—he didn't care about them! [*Feebly.*] He wasn't a god. He was a man. For whom everything was of the body, for the body! That's all! Again, the body! [*Screaming.*] This body is a traitor! [*She is writhing with pain.*] I despise this body—and I love it! I hate it—but—it's all you have, in the end, isn't it? It will be there. It will be yours. Where will it go without you? And where will you go if you reject it? Don't be ungrateful. It was your body that once burnt and gave you a moment so beautiful, so blissful, so near to heaven! Have you forgotten? It took you high, high, high above yourself into a place like paradise. Will you deny it? And now it carries within it the witness of that time— a tender little bud—of what will be a lisping, laughing, dancing little life—my son—my whole existence! I want my body now for him—for him alone. [*Shuts her eyes and mutters in mortal pain.*] He must have a mother... a father to call his own—a house—to be looked after—he must have a good name!

[*Darkness. Then light. The loud ticking of a watch. Benare is motionless in the dock as before. The others are all in their places.*]

KASHIKAR [*Lowering the hand which holds the watch in front of him*]. The time is up. The accused has no statement to make. In any case, it would be of no use. The cup of her crime is now full. Now—the judgement. Rokde, my wig, please.

[*Rokde hurriedly unpacks it and hands it to him. Kashikar puts it on and with all the grandeur of a solemn ritual, says*] Prisoner Miss Benare, pay the closest attention. The crimes you have committed are most terrible. There is no forgiveness for them. Your sin must be expiated. Irresponsibility must be chained down. Social customs, after all, are of supreme importance. Marriage is the very foundation of our society's stability. Motherhood must be sacred and pure. This court takes a serious view of your attempt to

dynamite all this. It is the firm opinion of this court that
your behaviour puts you beyond mercy. And, what is more,
the arrogance with which you conducted yourself in
society, having done all these things, that arrogance is the
most unforgivable thing of all. Criminals and sinners
should know their place. You have conducted yourself
above your station. The court expresses its indignation at
your presumptuousness. Moreover, the future of posterity
was entrusted to you. This is a very dreadful thing. The
morality which you have shown through your conduct was
the morality you were planning to impart to the youth of
tomorrow. This court has not an iota of doubt about it.
Hence not only today's, but tomorrow's society would have
been endangered by your misconduct. It must be said that
the school officials have done a work of merit in deciding
to remove you from your job. By the grace of God, it has
all been stopped in time. Neither you nor anyone else should
ever do anything like this again. No memento of your sin
should remain for future generations. Therefore this court
hereby sentences that you shall live. But the child in your
womb shall be destroyed.

BENARE. [*Writhing*]. No! No! No!—I won't let you do it—
I won't let it happen—I won't let it happen !

[*All are as still as statues. Benare comes sobbing to the
stool for the defence counsel. There she sits down, half
fainting. Then in paroxysms of torment, she collapses with
her head on the table, motionless. Stifled sobs come from
her.*

*Silence. By now it is quite dark in the hall. There is a noise
of someone opening the door. All start and look towards
it. The door quietly opens little by little. A line of light
comes in through it. Two or three faces look round.*]

FIRST FACE. [*Looking curiously at everyone in the hall*]. Has
the show begun ? The Living Courtroom ?

[*Everyone is startled to the realization. Consciousness dawns
afresh. Samant puts on the lights. Everyone quickly returns
to normal.*]

SAMANT. [*Getting up and going forward*]. Oh ? No, no, not

now—but it will, soon. But plesae wait outside. Come on
—five minutes—come on. [*He takes them out somehow.*]

KARNIK. Well! It's really late, you know.

MRS KASHIKAR. Goodness, I just didn't realize the time!

PONKSHE. What's the time? It's quite dark.

KASHIKAR. Rokde, it's your job to look after the timing of
the show. What were you doing all this time? Useless
fellow!

SUKHATME. Let him be, Kashikar. We had some good fun!
Felt just like fighting a real case!

KASHIKAR. Come on. Get ready quickly, everyone...come
on...

PONKSHE. I am always ready—

[*He points to Benare. They are all arrested. Silent, serious.
They gather round the motionless Benare.*].

MRS KASHIKAR [*Stroking the garland in her hair*]. She's
taken it really to heart. How sensitive the child is!

KASHIKAR. You're telling me. She's taking it much too much
to heart. After all it was—

SUKHATME. Just a game! What else? A game! That's all!

PONKSHE. A mere game!

KARNIK. Benare, come on, get up. It's time for the show.
The show must go on.

MRS KASHIKAR [*Shaking her*]. Do get up, Benare. The show
must start on time. Come on now. Look, it was all untrue.
It would hardly be true, would it?

[*Samant has entered.*]

PONKSHE. Samant, please arrange for some tea. The lady
needs some tea.

SAMANT. Yes.

KASHIKAR. [*Taking off his wig as he gets up. He notices the
bottle of* TIK-20 *in front of him on the table. For a moment, he stays looking at it with staring eyes. Then, removing his gaze, to the others*]. Come on... Come on—come
and wash and dress up—enough playing about! Now to
business! Come on.

[*All withdraw with silent steps into the next room, in a
herd behind him. Benare on the stage, motionless. Samant*

*by the door watching her. Embarrassed, he comes diffi-
dently in from one side and quietly picks up the bright
green cloth parrot that he had put there earlier, from the
luggage on the dais. He starts going back towards the door.
Then, unable to restrain himself, he stops some distance
from Benare. Looking at her, he is overcome by feeling.
He can't think what to do. He calls out indistinctly,
'Miss...' but she does not hear. He is even more embarrassed. Since there is nothing else he can do, gently,
affectionately, and with great respect he puts the green
cloth parrot in front of her, from a distance. Exit.
Benare feebly stirs a little. Then gives up the effort. The
bright green cloth parrot is near her. From somewhere
unseen, her own voice is heard singing softly.]*

      The parrot to the sparrow said,
      'Why, oh why, are your eyes so red?'
      'Oh, my dear friend, what shall I say?
      Someone has stolen my nest away.'
      Sparrow, sparrow, poor little sparrow...
      'Oh, brother crow, oh, brother crow,
      Were you there? Did you see it go?'
      'No, I don't know. I didn't see.
      What are your troubles to do with me?'
      O sparrow, sparrow, poor little sparrow ...

[Light on Benare only. The rest of the stage in darkness.]

CURTAIN